THE TUTTLE TWINS GUIDE TO
TRUE CONSPIRACIES

BY CONNOR BOYACK

© 2023 The Tuttle Twins Holding Co.

All rights reserved.

No graphic, visual, electronic, film, microfilm, tape recording, or any other means may be used to reproduce in any form, without prior written permission of the author, except in the case of brief passages embodied in critical reviews and articles.

ISBN 979-8-88688-011-3

Boyack, Connor, author.
Stanfield, Elijah, illustrator.
Hague, Katie, editor.
The Tuttle Twins Guide to True Conspiracies / Connor Boyack.

Cover design by Elijah Stanfield
Edited and typeset by Connor Boyack

Printed in the United States

10 9 8 7 6 5 4 3 2

The List of CONSPIRACIES

Nayirah and the Iraq War 1
Operation Mockingbird 13
Operation Paperclip 25
Gulf of Tonkin 35
Operation Sea-Spray 47
Project MK-Ultra 57
The Tuskegee Experiment 67
Operation Fast and Furious 77
Operation Popeye 87
Operation Northwoods 97
Sugar/Fat Studies 107
The Great Reset 117
Operation Ajax 131
Social Media Manipulation 143
Poisoned Booze 153
Unconstitutional Surveillance 163
COINTELPRO 177
Hunter Biden's Laptop 189
A New Pearl Harbor 199
The Creature from Jekyll Island 219

Have you ever seen a magician performing a magic trick? They are super fun to watch, and a good one will leave you wondering how it actually happened.

One tool that most magicians use is called misdirection—the act of drawing your attention to something unimportant (like their other hand or an object in front of you). Why would they do this?

Misdirection is used to distract you from what the magician is doing—the actual trick. By looking at something unimportant, you're less likely to focus on what's actually important. It's an act of deception to fool you into believing something is real that actually isn't. And it works very well—people can be very gullible, and they are susceptible to having their attention manipulated by others.

Sadly, tricks like these aren't just used by magicians. They are also used by those in power who want to get away with their conspiracies and corruption without people like you being aware of them. Their success relies on keeping you distracted and in the dark. So what can the average person do about this to stop it from happening?

Like with all our work, it starts with education. If we don't know what's real and true, then we won't be able to figure out the right solutions to the many problems in our world.

As it turns out, many people believe things that simply aren't true! They believe what they were told by the media, or what the government said, or what they read in an official report. But these people often lie. Many world events feature true conspiracies and happened in a different way than what the public now thinks.

Our goal in the chapters ahead is to help you realize just how frequently misdirection happens in our world today. We want you to realize how often our own government has conspired to do bad things, so that together we can stop it from happening in the future. We need to learn these truths if we're going to fight for a freer future.

Ready to begin?

—The Tuttle Twins

NAYIRAH
and the Iraq War

A 15-year-old's tearful testimony swayed a nation, but secrets lurked behind her words, igniting a war based on deception.

It was October 1990. The cloudy autumn air was warm as members of the Congressional Human Rights Caucus walked up the steps of the Capitol and made their way to their seats. President George H. W. Bush had been pushing Congress to authorize the United States to enter the conflict between Kuwait and its invading neighbor, Iraq, but so far he hadn't had much success in convincing them that US military action was warranted. He hoped the testimony the caucus members were about to hear would help change their minds.

As they sipped their coffee and shuffled their papers, their attention shifted to a young lady approaching the podium. She was small and thin with deep olive skin and dark, almond-shaped eyes. Her brown hair was pulled back in a single braid down her back, and she wore a white sweater with a black collar.

With a quivering voice, Nayirah began her testimony. She held back tears as she detailed how her summer vacation took a terrible turn when the Iraqi army forced their way into Kuwait City. The caucus members were in awe of her bravery as she recalled how her older sister, with her newborn baby, had escaped just in time, but how she, at only fifteen years old, had volunteered to stay in the occupied city to help at the local hospital.

They were sickened as she detailed how she was forced to stand by helplessly as Iraqi soldiers unplugged the oxygen supply, removed premature babies from their lifesaving incubators, and callously left them on the cold floor to die. She explained that they then took the incubators and shipped them back to Iraq, leaving the ravished city without lifesaving equipment.

As she continued, the committee learned that her friends had been brutally tortured too. She and her family had to dodge gunfire and suffer physical and verbal abuse—often actually running for their lives—as they fled Kuwait. Eventually, they made their way to the safety of the United States.

News channels all across the country aired her testimony. Americans were deeply impacted by what they heard. Politicians, including President Bush, were outraged, citing Nayirah's testimony repeatedly in their calls for military action against Iraq.

In August 1990, two months prior to Nayirah's testimony, only 17 percent of Americans said they supported US involvement in the clash between Saddam Hussein's Iraq and Kuwait. Just two months after her testimony, nearly half of Americans thought the United States needed to act, and in January 1991, Congress voted to authorize the deployment of American troops to fight against Iraq. The Senate passed their resolution by a margin of only five votes; seven senators cited Nayirah's testimony as directly impacting their decision to vote in favor of going to war.

Things Aren't Always What They Seem

Nayirah's harrowing story was shared by human rights organizations and governments around the world. Her bravery was heralded far and wide. There was just one problem.

Everything she said was a lie.

Nayirah's story began to unravel when it was revealed that her last name wasn't being kept secret to protect her from potential harm. Her full name was Nayirah Al-Sabah, and her father was… the Kuwaiti ambassador to the United States!

Naturally, some journalists had questions about this story—not everybody accepted it as true. And as questions were asked, without good answers in response, Nayirah's story began to fall apart. When human rights groups entered the Al Adan Hospital after the war ended, they found the NICU intact. There was no evidence showing Iraqi soldiers had done what they had been accused of. As Nayirah's narrative came crashing down, the real story began to emerge.

On August 11, 1990, just nine days after the Iraqi invasion of Kuwait, a group organized by the Kuwaiti government called Citizens for a Free Kuwait sent $10.8 million to the American public relations firm Hill & Knowlton. Their goal was to drum up support for US intervention in the war. They knew they had a much better chance at ousting the occupying Iraqi army if the United States entered the fray.

So the best and brightest minds at Hill & Knowlton began coaching the ambassador's daughter and arranging for her appearance before the congressional committee. They taught Nayirah what to say. They coached her on how to hold her hands when she spoke, what gestures to make, when to cry, and when to speak with sternness. Like an actress practicing for an important performance, Nayirah spent countless hours practicing her lines and rehearsing her movements. When it was time for the show, her acting paid off—her performance was very convincing.

It is still unknown just how much President George H.W. Bush knew about Nayirah's true identity. What has been verified is that Democratic Senator Tom Lantos, who chaired the Congressional Human Rights Caucus, knew who Nayirah was but chose not to tell his fellow committee members. What is certain is that the president wanted Congress to authorize a war against Saddam Hussein, and he used Nayirah's testimony several times in speeches and meetings to drum up support for his cause.

President Bush got his war, and a decade later George W. Bush followed in his father's footsteps, once again sending US soldiers to war with Iraq.

Nayirah never spoke publicly again. She disappeared from the public eye just as quickly as she had appeared, and no one was ever held responsible for fabricating her ten-million-dollar tall tale or the wars that followed because of it.

Cui Bono?

It is fair to say the people of Kuwait benefited by not having their country permanently annexed by Iraq. Saddam Hussein was a brutal dictator who oppressed his own people and sought to control the Kuwaiti people as well. The international community feared that failure to contain Hussein after his invasion of Kuwait would embolden him, possibly even resulting in him invading other neighboring countries and causing a "destabilization" in the Middle East.

But was it our fight to fight? And why did the United States choose *this* dictator and *this* conflict when examples of harsh rulers and acts of aggression are abundant all around the world?

Military writers and historians call the Gulf War a booming success. They tout the shortness of the war as an example of the swiftness with which the US military was able to meet a foe and vanquish them with relatively little loss of life or equipment. It's true that conflict was short—a mere forty-three days of which only about one hundred hours were ground combat. But calculating the actual length and loss of life and equipment varies, depending on how far we are willing to "zoom out" on the lens through which we are looking at this war.

Military leaders cite the Gulf War as a turning point in US warfighting. It was the first conflict in which all branches of service fought as a unified, centrally commanded force and not as individual, branch-specific operators. The lessons, they say, helped shape the US military into a force that was able to respond to the events of 9/11 and the following decades of continuous warfighting in multiple theaters. They view the Gulf War as a live-fire training exercise that prepared the military for the types of battle they would see in coming years.

But there are many who wonder if we would have avoided the prolonged and costly wars in the decades since if we had simply left Kuwait and its ally neighbors to fight a regional battle against a local aggressor. Surely, they would have been able to remove Saddam to his proper borders within his own country and hold him there. How many American and allied lives have been lost in wars and conflicts committed to using the Gulf War as a template and an encouragement?

In the years following Nayirah's testimony, the expansion of the US military and its defense industry exploded to never before seen size and scope. In 2021, the United States spent more than $800 billion on defense. War has become a multi-billion-dollar industry, and many see the United States as having become hawkish—circling the globe with an eye for conflicts to involve itself in. War, it seems, became a sort of business to be planned and managed by bureaucrats and politicians with an eye on their investment portfolios and their retirement accounts. The human cost of war has been practically ignored.

Would this have happened if Nayirah hadn't testified and US public opinion hadn't been shifted to support intervention in a conflict between two small countries half a world away?

Why Does This Matter?

Since the Gulf War, the ease with which the United States has committed troops and resources to armed conflict has only increased. The Gulf War acted as a type of warfighting Pandora's box—loosing the power and might of the US military (and the US dollar) and applying it to seemingly endless conflicts and causes.

There is always a plea from one small country or another asking for an international commitment of troops or funding to its regional conflict. At the writing of this book, the small country of Ukraine, led by a professional actor and comedian-turned-president, has succeeded in securing over $75 billion in funding from the United States to assist in its conflict with Russia. There have been claims that many of the videos used to increase support for Ukraine—videos showing bombed-out neighborhoods and civilian casualties—have actually been created in Hollywood-style studios and circulated to news networks around the world in order to garner international sympathy and support for Ukraine.

One thing is certain: once a tool of manipulation is proven effective, it is unlikely it will be abandoned. If, clear back in 1990, governments knew that all it took was a sympathetic actor, a little coaching, and a chunk of money to change public opinion to favor committing US assets and lives to a war that wasn't theirs to fight, it is safe to assume these methods are still being used today and will be used in the future.

What We Learned

1. The government will knowingly spread lies if it helps them get the public to agree to something.

2. Manipulating voters' emotions will shift their opinions.

3. When politicians lie, they often suffer no consequences.

4. Foreign governments use money and influence to shape American policy.

5. Politicians keep secrets not only from the public, but from each other, in order to manipulate a story or shape a narrative.

Nayirah's Testimony

Given to the United States Congressional
Human Rights Caucus

October 10, 1990

Mr. Chairman, and members of the committee, my name is Nayirah and I just came out of Kuwait. My mother and I were in Kuwait on August 2nd for a peaceful summer holiday. My older sister had a baby on July 29th and we wanted to spend some time in Kuwait with her.

I only pray that none of my 10th grade classmates had a summer vacation like I did. I may have wished sometimes that I can be an adult, that I could grow up quickly. What I saw happening to the children of Kuwait and to my country has changed my life forever, has changed the life of all Kuwaitis, young and old, mere children or more.

My sister with my five-day-old nephew traveled across the desert to safety. There is no milk available for the baby in Kuwait. They barely escaped when their car was stuck in the desert sand and help came from Saudi Arabia.

I stayed behind and wanted to do something for my country. The second week after invasion, I volunteered at the AlIdar (phonetic rendering) Hospital with 12 other women who wanted to help as well. I was the youngest volunteer. The "other" women were from 20 to 30 years old.

While I was there, I saw the Iraqi soldiers come into the hospital with guns. They took the babies out of the incubators, took the incubators and left the children to die on the cold floor. It was horrifying. I could not help but think of my nephew who was born premature and might have died that day as well. After I left the hospital, some of my friends and I distributed flyers condemning the Iraqi invasion until we were warned we might be killed if the Iraqis saw us.

The Iraqis have destroyed everything in Kuwait. They stripped the supermarkets of food, the pharmacies of medicine, the factories of medical supplies, ransacked their houses and tortured neighbors and friends.

I saw and talked to a friend of mine after his torture and release by the Iraqis. He is 22 but he looked as though he could have been an old man. The Iraqis dunked his head into a swimming pool until he almost drowned. They pulled out his fingernails and then played [sic] electric shocks to sensitive private parts of his body. He was lucky to survive.

If an Iraqi soldier is found dead in the neighborhood, they burn to the ground all the houses in the general vicinity and would not let firefighters come until the only ash and rubble was left.

The Iraqis were making fun of President Bush and verbally and physically abusing my family and me on our way out of Kuwait. We only did so because life in Kuwait became unbearable. They have forced us to hide, burn or destroy everything identifying our country and our government.

I want to emphasize that Kuwait is our mother and the Emir our father. We repeated this on the roofs of our houses in Kuwait until the Iraqis began shooting at us, and we shall repeat it again. I am glad I am 15, old enough to remember Kuwait before Saddam Hussein destroyed it and young enough to rebuild it.

Thank you.

Operation
MOCKINGBIRD

In post-war America, as families relished the comforts of daily life, a hidden web ensnared the nation's conscience. The CIA's clandestine endeavors entangled journalists and artists to puppeteer public sentiment.

How America's Most Powerful
News Media Worked Hand
in Glove with the Central Intelligence
Agency and Why the
Church Committee Covered It Up

THE CIA AND THE MEDIA

BY CARL BERNSTEIN

n 1953, Joseph Alsop, then one of America's leading syndicated columnists, went to the Philippines to cover an election. He did not go because he was asked to do so by his syndicate. He did not go because he was asked to do so by the newspapers that

The 1950s and '60s were an idyllic time in America. The Second World War was fading into the past and taking with it all the memories of hardship and suffering. There was a general feeling of hope and a promise of prosperity covering most of the country. Husbands went to work in tailored suits and came home to adoring children, tidy homes, and loving wives. There was finally time again for leisure, art, and music, plus movies were flooding even the smallest towns with culture and excitement.

But perhaps the most exciting thing of all was the availability, and affordability, of the black and white television. There had never been an invention that swept the nation and found its way into nearly every home more quickly than this modern communication and entertainment marvel. After supper was eaten and the children were bathed and tucked neatly into their matching beds, mother and father would sit down in front of the television and listen to the trusted news reporter relay the events of the day. It felt good to be home. It felt good to be informed. There was a feeling of belonging, importance, and having your feet planted on solid ground with a clear and accurate picture of the world around you while understanding your place in it.

It felt good to be an American.

Things Aren't Always What They Seem

Beginning in the 1950s, the Central Intelligence Agency (CIA) started recruiting students, artists, and journalists to influence the attitudes and opinions of average citizens by controlling what ideas, events, and perspectives they were exposed to in news and entertainment.

Millions of dollars were paid to individuals and organizations that agreed to help the CIA in their mission to control the way Americans thought about the world around them. Sometimes the stories promoted were entirely false—fabrications conjured up in a dim corner of an office at CIA headquarters in Langley, Virginia. Other times, the story was true, but the "spin" put on it (the way it was presented) pushed the person reading or listening to see the story from a very specific perspective and come to a very specific conclusion—the conclusion the government had decided best served their purposes.

Designed under the guise of protecting American interests from the threat of communism, Operation Mockingbird turned the propaganda-making might of the US intelligence community inward—focusing it not on enemies abroad but instead on domestic targets: average Americans. The masterminds of Mockingbird were Frank Wisner and Allen W. Dulles (the first civilian director of the CIA). They recruited well-known and trusted American journalists into a news and media-controlling civilian army. Additionally, the CIA funded student groups from college campuses, cultural organizations, magazine editors, and even artists to "unofficially" work for them in their efforts to manipulate and control the clueless populace.

In February 1967, the *New York Times* published an article claiming to have proof of the CIA making payments to some student organizations. A few other articles were published, but they were mostly ignored. In 1973, the *Washington Star* published a report that more than thirty

American journalists were being paid by the CIA. The CIA refused to disclose their names, claiming that to do so would endanger the writers' and reporters' lives. This led many to wonder why, if they weren't actually working for the CIA, it could be dangerous for their names to be known.

Finally, Congress took notice, and a series of congressional investigations followed. The Senate organized the Church Committee—charged with investigating the CIA, FBI, IRS, and NSA for any domestic "government operations and potential abuses." For all the morally and ethically questionable things the CIA and other intelligence agencies did (and do!), it was still against the law for them to operate against citizens of the United States within the country. Senator Frank Church and his colleagues wrote:

> In examining the CIA's past and present use of the U.S. media, the Committee finds two reasons for concern. The first is the potential, inherent in covert media operations, for manipulating or incidentally misleading the American public. The second is the damage to the credibility and independence of a free press which may be caused by covert relationships with the U.S. journalists and media organizations.

Meanwhile, the CIA continued to promise Congress and the American people that they would never do anything that would risk influencing domestic public opinion, either directly or indirectly. They claimed they had a standing policy specifically prohibiting the placement of propaganda in the American media. They didn't mention their standing policy of *ignoring their own policies*.

By 1975, the story began to unravel, and the CIA admitted to Congress that they had, for decades, been actively manipulating the American people by using the mainstream media to redirect the thoughts and opinions of American citizens. They acknowledged that they worked with journalists and other media personalities to distort truth in order to fit specific agendas. There were no big announcements made to the American public—most people never even knew that their government had been purposely and actively manipulating them through radio, television, and entertainment for most of their lives.

It wasn't until a *Rolling Stone* article in 1977 that news of the CIA's misdeeds went mainstream. Carl Bernstein's investigative work titled "The CIA and the Media" charged that the CIA "has secretly bankrolled numerous foreign press services, periodicals and newspapers—both in English and foreign language—which provided excellent cover for CIA operatives." He found that journalists not only wrote the stories the CIA asked them to and presented them to Americans as fact, but they often had very close relationships with intelligence officers. They willingly shared their notebooks and actively collaborated with them to disseminate elaborate lies or to put twists on real stories that made them appear entirely different than they actually were.

He also charged that the CIA was not merely manipulating the foreign press, but the domestic press as well, and went as far as to name the networks, publications, and people who had aided the CIA in their efforts. CBS, *Time*, the *New York Times*, the *Louisville Courier-Journal*, ABC, Reuters, NBC, and the Copley News Service were all working for the CIA and being compensated very well financially for their troubles.

Although newly appointed Director of Central Intelligence George H.W. Bush ordered the CIA, in 1976, to cease domestic media manipulation and barred government agencies from "entering into any paid or contractual relationships with any full-time or part-time news correspondent accredited by any United States news service, newspaper, periodical, radio or television network or station," many still suspect that this is happening today.

One estimate suggests that the US government, through Mockingbird, spent hundreds of millions of dollars a year—for more than twenty years—in its efforts to shape and direct the feelings, thoughts, opinions, and tastes of Americans. They were, for the most part, successful in accomplishing their goals.

Cui Bono?

Throughout the world, there are totalitarian governments that strictly limit and control the ability of their people to access news and information. In China and North Korea, Western media is prohibited, and controls are placed on the internet to block unapproved content. Similarly, many Middle Eastern countries strictly limit the types of art, music, news, and media that are accessible by their citizens. It's easy for Americans to look at these heavy-handed approaches to controlling the way people think, and what they know, and judge themselves lucky to be free from such restrictions. But are we really?

It's easier to fool someone than to convince them that they have been fooled, and it seems that the intelligence community has counted on that quirk of human nature as they lay their secret plans. Why use heavy-handed force to ensure your citizenry only sees the world you've approved for them—risking rebellion or regime change amid charges of being antidemocratic—if you can instead convince them that they are free while controlling what they see, hear, and believe? Are people any more free if they willingly place the shackles on their own feet and hand the key to their jailer than if the jailer does the shackling?

Mockingbird shaped the way an entire generation of people grew up to see themselves, their country, and the world around them. No source of information was left unmanipulated. Yet, most of those people still don't know that their worldviews were carefully crafted by men and women who went to great lengths to make them believe they were freethinkers while controlling their most formative experiences.

The people who were manipulated by Mockingbird went on to assume roles in government, business, media, art, and entertainment where they willingly and ignorantly became mouthpieces for government propaganda. The CIA no longer needed to spend billions of dollars to manipulate Americans—they had created an army of civilian operatives through their earlier efforts, and now all they had to do was keep feeding them the "official story"—whatever they decided that story should be—and resting comfortably in the knowledge that their "truth" would fill the airwaves, art galleries, history books, and newspapers.

Why Does This Matter?

What have we seen in recent years that could be compared to Mockingbird? Have there been any times when it seemed that celebrities, artists, musicians, journalists, and media personalities were all talking about the same things or pushing the same stories or the same versions of events?

Knowing that Mockingbird was real helps us to look at the world around us differently—making us more thoughtful about the things we see and hear in the different types of media we consume and in the news we read and watch. Although the secret program was officially (and allegedly) shuttered in the late 1970s, its influence is still being felt. Most journalists, musicians, artists, and celebrities quickly fall in lockstep with the government when a "bad guy" has been identified or a narrative is being promoted.

During the COVID-19 pandemic, not only did virtually all sources of information and entertainment support what the government was mandating and saying, but those who questioned the "official" story were attacked, deplatformed, fired, disparaged, or in other ways silenced or punished. Are people really free if they can't talk about their own health and the health of their loved ones without being persecuted?

Mark Twain was right: "Whenever you find yourself on the side of the majority, it is time to pause and reflect."

What We Learned

1. The government has a vested interest in controlling the way a country's population views and interprets the world around them, and they are willing to spend hundreds of millions of dollars to influence it.

2. Intelligence agencies often operate entirely outside the control and awareness of elected representatives. They are simply not accountable to anyone until something they are doing is discovered and people begin asking questions and demanding accountability.

3. Even when it is proven that intelligence agencies have operated against the very people whose interests they are tasked with protecting, there are often no consequences, and worse—the average citizen often doesn't pay attention or care.

4. Celebrities, entertainers, and media personalities will sacrifice their credibility and their morals for money and status. They will lie to the people who look up to and trust them if it means increased fame and fortune.

Congressional Report

From the Select Committee to Study Governmental Operations with Respect to Intelligence Activities

April 26, 1976

About half of the some 50 CIA relationships with the U.S. media were paid relationships, ranging from salaried operatives working under journalistic cover, to U.S. journalists serving as "independent contractors" for the CIA and being paid regularly for their services, to those who receive only occasional gifts and reimbursements from the CIA.

More than a dozen United States news organizations and commercial publishing houses formerly provided cover for CIA agents abroad. A few of these organizations were unaware that they provided this cover.

Although the variety of the CIA relationships with the U.S. media makes a systematic breakdown of them almost impossible, former CIA Director Colby has distinguished among four types of relationships. These are :

(1) Staff of general circulation, U.S. news organizations;

(2) Staff of small, or limited circulation, U.S. publications;

(3) Free-lance, stringers, propaganda writers, and employees of U.S. publishing houses;

(4) Journalists with whom CIA maintains unpaid, occasional, covert contact.

While the CIA did not provide the names of its media agents or the names of the media organizations with which they are connected, the Committee reviewed summaries of their relationships and work with the CIA. Through this review the Committee found that as of February 1976:

(1) The first category... appears to be virtually phased out. In at least one case the journalistic functions assumed by a CIA staff officer for cover purposes grew to a point where the officer concluded that he could not satisfactorily serve the requirements of both his (unwitting) U.S. media employers and the CIA, and therefore resigned from the CIA. He maintained contact, however, with the CIA and continued... to report to the CIA.

(2) Of the less than ten relationships with writers for small, or limited circulation, U.S. publications, such as trade journals or newsletters, most are for cover purposes.

(3) The third, and largest, category of CIA relationships with the U.S. media includes free-lance journalists... and agents working under cover as employees of U.S. publishing houses abroad... Most are paid by the CIA, and virtually all are witting; few, however, of the news organizations to which they contribute are aware of their CIA relationships.

(4) The fourth category of covert relationships resembles the kind of contact that journalists have with any other department of the U.S. Government in the routine performance of their journalistic duties. No money changes hands. The relationships are usually limited to occasional lunches, interviews, or telephone conversations during which information would be exchanged or verified. The difference, of course, is that the relationships are covert. The journalist either volunteers or is requested by the CIA to provide some sort of information about people with whom he is in contact.

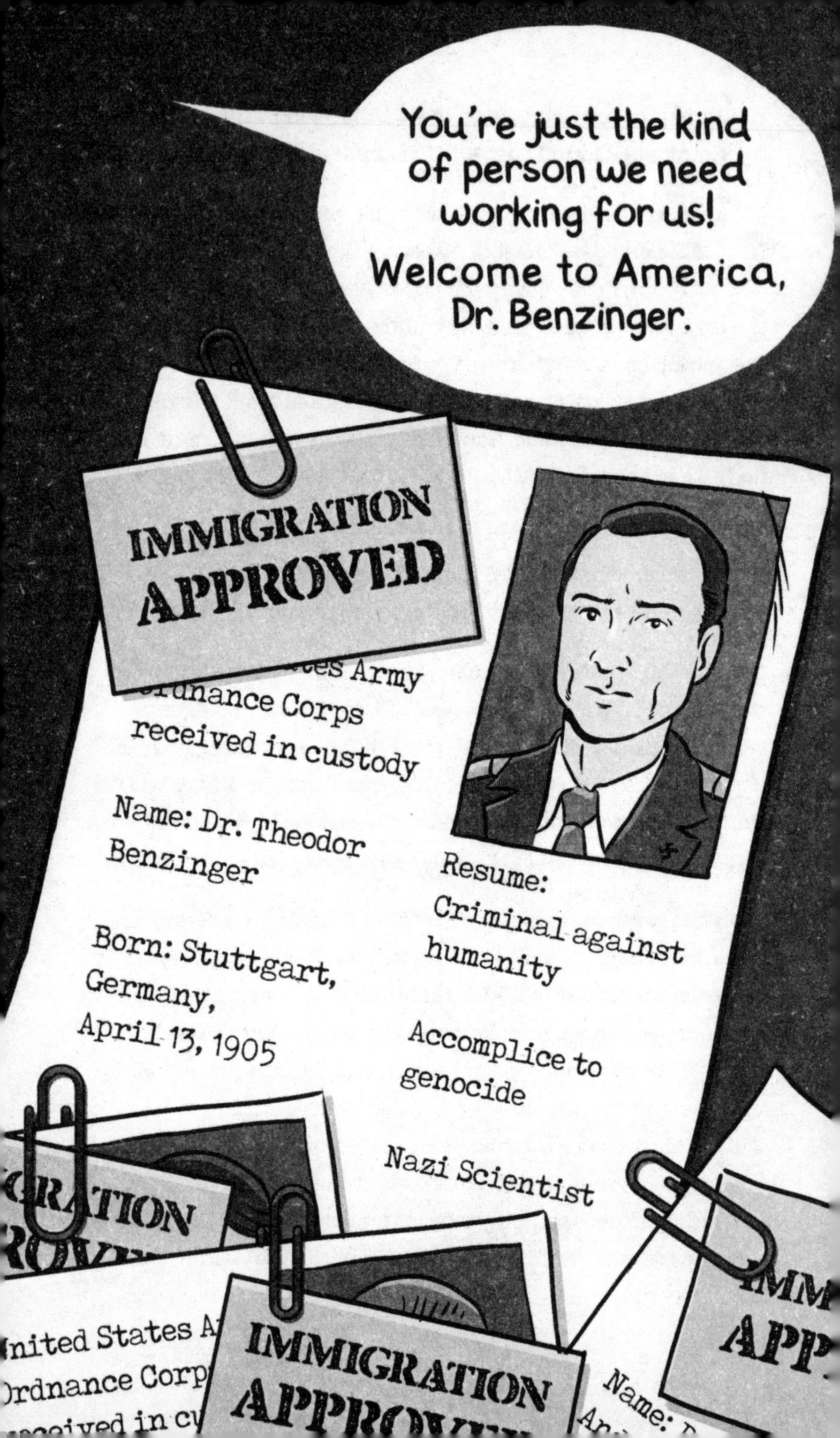

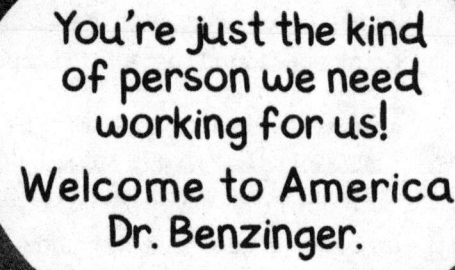

Operation
PAPERCLIP

Behind an illustrious career lies a secret: a scientist's chilling past in Nazi camps and the US government's covert operation to protect him.

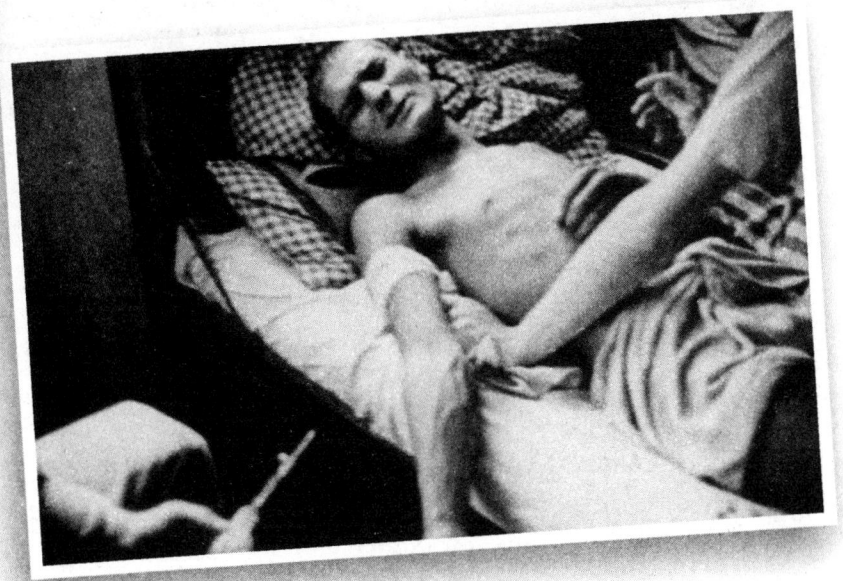

On a cool autumn day, as burnt orange and yellow leaves let loose their hold and fluttered to the ground from high atop trees backed by a bright blue sky, a brilliant scientist, father, and husband lay in his bed. He was surrounded by his loved ones who had gathered to be with him in his final days. At ninety-four, his imminent passing didn't come as a shock to his family and friends, but as they watched him peacefully slumbering, they reflected on his rich life and all that he meant to them. They were sure going to miss him when he was gone.

Born in Stuttgart, Germany, in 1905, Dr. Theo Benzinger was raised in a home that valued intelligence and education. He was a studious pupil, even in his youth, and was known to be a hard worker with a quick mind and a determined nature. His hard work paid off, and in time he earned a medical degree from the University of Freiburg. His qualifications allowed him to immigrate to the United States where he was awarded a position at the Naval Medical Research Institute in Bethesda, Maryland, and by 1955 he was married with four children and had become a naturalized US citizen.

His research focused on medical studies surrounding the human body's ability to regulate temperature, eventually developing the technologies that led to the invention of the ear thermometer. Dr. Benzinger was particularly interested in the operation of blood vessels and their expansion and contraction while under changing pressure and temperatures. He conducted high-altitude physiological studies aimed at helping pilots better navigate and survive the extreme conditions they encountered in ever-changing air combat situations. He spent his whole life in the research and development of medical and scientific marvels—even expanding the second law of thermodynamics.

On October 26, 1999, Dr. Theo Benzinger passed peacefully, leaving behind his loving wife, adoring children and a legacy of contributions that improved the daily lives of others—proof the "American Dream" was available for all who would spend their lives in hard work and dedication to the betterment of their fellow man.

Things Aren't Always What They Seem

It is true that Theo Benzinger was an accomplished doctor and scientist. It is also true that his research increased the medical and scientific body of knowledge and meaningful advancements were built on the foundations of his work. But what his colleagues didn't know was that much of his early research wasn't conducted in traditional ways—in fact, much of what he learned about the human body was discovered under bone-chilling circumstances.

Dr. Benzinger's fascination with the human body and its responses to trauma, high stress, and extreme pressure began long before his immigration to the United States. After medical school, he served in the German military where he became the director of the Luftwaffe's aviation medicine center. There, he studied pressure adaptation at altitude, desalination, thermoregulation, and respiratory physiology. Eventually his work led him to Dachau, the first of what would become a network of over 40,000 work and internment camps established by the Nazis during the Second World War.

The structure and methods used at Dachau formed the blueprint for other concentration camps, including the now-notorious Auschwitz and Ravensbrück camps, where over a million prisoners were murdered over the course of the war. A survivor of the Dachau camp, Max Mannheimer, said that although many people knew of the camp, early on, "They did not know about the torture and medical experiments that happened here." Dachau was used largely by doctors and scientists to create poisonous gases, study torture techniques, and experiment on the effects of compression and decompression on the human body for high-altitude aviation operations. They performed their grotesque research on prisoners—men, women, and children—who had been taken from their homes and families, loaded onto trains, and shipped to prisons without ever having done anything wrong. Dr. Benzinger led these experiments.

As Allied forces moved into Germany and began liberating camps, word began to spread of the atrocities being carried out in the name of "science." Many Nazi scientists were arrested, and twenty-three of them were tried in what became known as the Doctors Trial—a hearing held in Nuremberg where the details of the medical experiments and torture committed by high-ranking Nazis on prisoners were brought to light and those who had participated were brought to justice. Believing the guilty had been punished, the world began to heal and rebuild.

Dr. Theodore Benzinger was one of the scientists arrested for his crimes at Dachau in 1946. His name was included in the original Doctors Trial list of defendants, but something strange happened between his arrest and the trial. Not only did his name disappear from the official court records, but *he* disappeared as well, resurfacing eventually in Bethesda, Maryland, as a well-credentialed doctor and researcher working at the Naval Medical Research Institute.

And he wasn't the only one.

As time passed, a terrible, hidden truth came to light: the United States had cut secret deals with at least 1,600 of the worst criminals and murderers the world has ever known—giving them new lives in the United States, protecting them from the consequences of their evil deeds, and putting them on the government payroll in exchange for them sharing the medical and technological discoveries they made during the war—discoveries made by performing medical tests and procedures on weak and helpless prisoners of war. This effort was named Operation Paperclip.

Cui Bono?

In the name of science, the US government turned a blind eye to the atrocities committed by Nazis during and after the war and instead installed them in positions of influence and power within the United States. Over 1,600 Nazis and their families were eventually brought to the states in the years following the war. The American public was unaware this was happening, but it's easy to imagine that most Americans would have rejected amnesty being given to the very men many of their husbands, sons, and brothers had died fighting. Government leaders knew this, and so the program was kept a secret.

The idea was that these brilliant (albeit immoral) scientists would give the United States an advantage in the post-war world. Was it *really* in the best interest of humankind to let these people serve long prison sentences for their crimes, or was it, officials wondered, better to use the knowledge they gained from their inhumane, human experiments to "help" the world advance?

Soon, the Cold War would begin, and with that came the space race with Russia. Many of the top Nazi scientists and engineers were put to work in the new US space program. In fact, Wernher von Braun, once notorious for developing the V-2 rocket that killed tens of thousands of American and Allied forces during the war, became the director of NASA's Marshall Space Flight Center and was the chief architect of the Saturn V launch vehicle.

Those in power justified their decision to protect bad people from the consequences of their actions by claiming it was for a higher good. After all, they reasoned, the terrible things had already been done, and it would be a shame to let all of this information they had go to waste. So they proceeded with their secret plan.

It would be interesting to know if the families of their victims or the soldiers who died fighting the Nazis thought amnesty for these scientific criminals actually served the "greater good."

Why Does This Matter?

The government had an opportunity to take advantage of discoveries made through very unethical experiments and tests. They weighed all of the reasons why it was wrong to wipe clean the pasts of people who had committed war crimes—having a clear understanding of the horrible things that they had done to other human beings—and they chose to proceed. This wasn't just one person in government, acting alone and without any accountability. It was many people who all worked together to locate, smuggle to the United States, and supply with new identities, some of the very worst people in the world at the time.

They believed "the ends justified the means." This saying is used to explain why someone would do something that is wrong in order to bring about an outcome that they believe is ultimately right or serves a "greater good." This justification is often used by people in positions of power, but is it really okay to do something bad so something good can (hopefully) come from it later? Should a person be killed because their organs are a match for an important, dying person? Obviously not, yet that is the type of flawed thinking that a "greater good" mentality justifies. Sure, the United States benefited from some of the discoveries made by Nazi doctors and scientists, but does that mean those discoveries—or maybe even better discoveries!—wouldn't have been made if these people had instead had to face judgment and punishment for the crimes they committed against others? Surely there was a way to invent the ear thermometer without torturing prisoners in a concentration camp.

And there is something else to consider. While time and resources were being spent on tracking down these scientists and building fake new lives for them, what lifesaving or world-improving work *wasn't* being done? This is called *opportunity cost*—the truth that whenever we pursue one thing, we are missing out on pursuing something else. What brilliant young scientists and doctors were overlooked while Nazi scientists and doctors were being sought after and given jobs? What technology do we not have today that we would have had if the government had chosen differently all those years ago?

Did the ends justify the means? Or, in other words, was it worth it to deceive the American people and forgive these Nazis—erasing their evil past and giving them good jobs— to gain the knowledge they had to offer? Probably not. Is the government still doing things that will anger and shock us when the truth finally comes out? Almost certainly.

What We Learned

1. Very bad people are often protected by the government if they are viewed as potentially useful.

2. Some advances in modern medicine and technology have come from experiments that purposely caused tremendous human suffering.

3. People in power often believe that terrible things are justifiable if they are for the "greater good." Of course, *they* decide what the greater good is.

Top Secret Memorandum

A proposal from the Secretary of State, approved by President Truman four days later

August 30, 1946

I am presenting for your approval a statement of United States policy on the interim exploitation of selected German and Austrian specialists in the United States.

Since shortly after V-E Day the War Department has operated a project known as "Paperclip," under which selected German scientists have been brought to this country under military custody for short-term exploitation. There remains in our zones of Germany and Austria a number of specialists whose knowledge and ability could be used to further our technology. General McNarney has reported that the services of many of these specialists may be lost to us unless steps are taken quickly to assure exploitation under favorable circumstances.

The statement provides for expanding "Paperclip" to include a total of between 800 and 1000 specialists. Since cooperation of the specialists is necessary to successful exploitation, provision is made for bringing members of specialists' families to this country, and for relaxing the formerly strict custody arrangements. The War Department would be responsible for custody and for excluding from the program persons with Nazi or militaristic records.

It is contemplated that at a later date selected persons would be granted regular status under the immigration laws.

This statement is based on recommendations of the Joint Chiefs of Staff, and has been approved by the State, War and Navy Departments. I recommend your approval.

Excuse me, Mr. President. The report was a mistake. There was no attack...
Don't bother me with the details, son. I've got a war to start...
PRESIDENT OF THE UNITED S
E PLURIBUS UNUM

Gulf of
TONKIN

Was the fuse of the Vietnam War lit falsely? Revelations hint at shadows of deceit and high-stakes manipulation in the corridors of power. The staggering human toll haunts the legacy of a conflict wrapped in layers of murky intrigue and mystery.

There was a clear blue sky with just a few puffy clouds dotting the horizon the morning of August 2, 1964, when over 300 men on board the USS *Maddox*, a US Navy destroyer on a patrol mission off the coast of Vietnam, awoke to alarms and shouts to man their battle stations. Although the United States wasn't at war, there was trouble brewing between Communist North Vietnam and their southern neighbors, and the United States had amped up its presence in the region. The *Maddox* had been in the area for a few weeks, running information gathering missions in international waters without incident, so the men were surprised to be suddenly called to action.

As they manned their posts, there came into view three small North Vietnamese torpedo boats. They were running with throttles wide open—closing the distance at breakneck speed. The captain had only a moment to decide what to do. He knew the torpedo boats had a range of one thousand feet and had to decide whether they were facing an attack before they got too much closer.

The enemy boats showed no sign of slowing. The captain was sure they planned to strike. He instructed his crew to open fire, and mere seconds later the Vietnamese captains fired as well. With quick thinking and quick maneuvering, the *Maddox* avoided a direct hit, and the torpedoes sailed harmlessly off into the open sea.

The attackers weren't as lucky. The superior firepower and range of the US destroyer made short work of the enemy boats. Several crew members were killed and more were wounded. All three torpedo boats were damaged beyond repair.

The *Maddox* relayed the events to headquarters, and the secretary of defense was put on high alert. Another unprovoked attack on a US ship could mean war. Surely, the North Vietnamese understood the dangerous position they were in and would stay away from the US fleet in the future.

But far from being subdued by the sinking of their torpedo boats, the North Vietnamese seemed to be emboldened. Just two days after the *Maddox* was attacked, under the cover of rough seas and low visibility, the torpedo boats were back! For two hours, the crew of the *Maddox* fired off rounds and zigzagged in evasive maneuvers—doing all they could to protect themselves and defend their ship against its attackers.

Finally, the assault stopped. The *Maddox* had again emerged victorious! But as the captain and crew celebrated their escape, a heaviness settled in the air. When the president learned that the North Vietnamese had attacked again, things were going to get very serious.

Things Aren't Always What They Seem

Things did, indeed, get serious. Within hours of the second attack, President Lyndon B. Johnson interrupted national television to make an announcement, describing an attack by North Vietnamese ships on two US Navy ships. Within thirty minutes of the second incident on August 4, Johnson began demanding retaliatory attacks against North Vietnam. Soon after, the Gulf of Tonkin Resolution was drafted and passed by Congress, giving the president authorization to deploy ground combat troops in Vietnam.

The Vietnam War raged on for almost twenty years and cost the lives of more than 58,000 US troops. Additionally, over a million North Vietnamese soldiers were killed,

200,000 South Vietnamese soldiers, and more than two million civilians in the North and South. The US military sprayed a chemical compound called Agent Orange all over the crops and jungles, and in rivers and lakes to destroy the food supply and kill the vegetation that provided cover for the movements of the North Vietnamese army.

Agent Orange turned out to be a deadly substance—leaving those who had come in contact with it with painful, lifelong ailments and causing birth defects, cancers, and eventual death. In addition to the fatalities of war, it is estimated that a million more soldiers, civilians, and children on both sides of the conflict suffered and died from exposure to this toxin.

For all this suffering and death, many Americans still believed that the Vietnam War was a just cause—that it had to be fought to protect American interests and to keep the Communist North Vietnamese from spreading their form of government forcefully on their southern neighbors. And besides, the North Vietnamese had brought this war on themselves when they attacked the *Maddox*.

But as time passed, some people who had been there that day began to speak out about what they saw—and what they *didn't see*—in the Gulf of Tonkin. The truth would cost the secretary of defense his credibility and bring shame to the United States and the office of the president.

There was no second attack on the *Maddox*. There weren't even any Vietnamese ships in the area when the alleged attack happened. All the zigzagging and shooting had been for nothing—an overreaction by the crew of the *Maddox* to bad weather, shoddy communications, tense nerves, and static that they misinterpreted as enemy "chatter." At best, it was a big mistake. The crew of the *Maddox* didn't have time to confirm what had happened before Johnson addressed the nation and declared North Vietnam the enemy. At worst, the president knew there was uncertainty about what had taken place, but he and his advisers decided to use the story of the second attack to justify going to war. After all, Johnson had a lot of reasons to push for US involvement in Vietnam.

First, with an election just around the corner, Johnson saw an opportunity to appear tough on communism and shore up support from voters who were concerned about the spread of Soviet power around the world. Second, there was considerable pressure from Defense Secretary Robert McNamara and other senior military officials to take decisive action against North Vietnam after the initial attack on the *Maddox*.

There are even indications that Johnson's administration may have deliberately exaggerated or even fabricated aspects of the story in order to gain public support for military action. For example, documents released years later demonstrated that evidence had been falsified in order to support the proposal of retaliation. Some documents were altered and other items were cherry picked to distort the truth and make the situation look like it was a set of repeated, intentional attacks.

There is also record of crew members from the *Maddox* initially reporting that no enemy boats or aircraft were in the region on August 4 and that faulty equipment and inexperienced crewmen led to false claims of ship sightings that day.

Cui Bono?

One thing that becomes clear as we study history—and particularly the history of war—is that it is rarely the people of any nation who benefit from armed conflict. This is a strange truth, since it is almost always "the well-being of the people" that government leaders use in their justification for going to war. They make appeals to the people of their own country asking them to spend large sums of money, allocate resources (often away from other things), and even commit the lives of their own young men and women to go someplace far away and "protect" or "liberate" or "defend" others.

The Vietnam War is an example of how military intervention often causes more harm than good and how those who do benefit are not the people who need the most help. US military leaders and government officials conspired to go to war with North Vietnam because they believed communism must be contained at all costs and allowing even one part of a nation to fall under Communist rule would pose a threat to the safety and prosperity of the whole world.

Were they right about the need for containment? Perhaps. Communism is a deadly ideology with a clear history of pain, suffering, despair, and death everywhere it has ever been tried. Protecting the world from communism is probably a noble goal, but how far should the United States have been willing to go to contain this lethal brand of government?

By the time the war was over, the United States was fiercely divided. So many young Americans had been sent to die in a conflict that many back at home weren't convinced was a righteous or winnable cause. Americans had been heroes in the Second World War—fighting valiantly alongside their allies from France and other countries to free the world from the grip of a man bent on taking it over and "cleansing" it of anyone who he saw as inferior. The American people supported the war because they believed that what they were fighting and sacrificing for was good.

Now, they were unconvinced, and as the war in Vietnam dragged on, the people at home became more and more angry with their government. Protests were common (and sometimes violent), and many soldiers were treated poorly when they came home. The war caused deep wounds in the hearts of the people of the United States that have taken many years to begin to heal.

What about the people of Vietnam? Did they at least benefit from the war waged to save them from their Communist neighbors to the north? It's true that they didn't fall under communist rule, but at what cost? It is estimated that millions of Vietnamese people died in, and as a result of, the war. Additionally, exposure to Agent Orange and other toxic chemicals sprayed on farmland, in the jungles, and along riverbanks is believed to have killed nearly a million people in the years following the war and led to a half million birth defects and permanent disabilities.

While there was a lot of confusion in the wake of the attack on the *Maddox*, it seems that some within the Johnson administration—particularly US Secretary of Defense Robert McNamara—were intentionally deceptive about what had happened because they believed that retaliation and war was for a good cause—to protect the world from communism. They thought if they could justify inserting themselves in a conflict between nations halfway across the world, they could deal a deadly blow to an ideology they rightfully believed was a danger to freedom and democracy. But they were wrong and, in the end, their deceit led to decades of misery and suffering for not just the people they claimed to be "saving," but their own people as well.

There were no winners in the Vietnam War.

Why Does This Matter?

Since the Vietnam War, the United States government has employed similarly dishonest methods to garner public support for war. For example, after the attacks on 9/11, even though there was no official tie to Iraq or Saddam Hussein, the United States invaded Iraq and ousted their president. Months of congressional testimony and near-constant media attention convinced Congress and most Americans that Saddam Hussein possessed "weapons of mass destruction"—chemical and biological weapons that could inflict mass casualties on civilian populations—and had to be stopped.

The United States Army invaded Iraq on March 20, 2003, in a mission they called *Shock and Awe*, which saw the might of the US arsenal unleashed on a country roughly the size of California. The United States and allied forces spent the next eight years setting up bases, chasing so-called terrorists, implementing a new government, and looking for the weapons. No weapons were ever found, but at least 150,000 (some estimates place this number at 600,000) Iraqis were killed, nearly 5,000 American soldiers lost their lives, and 32,000 Americans were wounded.

In this example and countless others, there were no consequences for wrongfully invading another country, toppling its government, and causing mass casualties. In fact, military leaders were promoted, and weapons manufacturers, politicians, and government contractors made billions of dollars. Having learned how easy it is to deceive people into supporting war, and knowing how profitable war can be to those who stand to benefit from it, it is likely that these same methods of deception will continue to be used in the future.

What We Learned

1. The government will rely on faulty intelligence and even fabricated stories as the justification for starting a war.

2. Those in positions of power don't always think through (or don't care about) the long-term consequences of the methods and means they use in war—causing lasting harm to natural resources and human life for generations after the conflict has ended.

3. Civilian casualties commonly outnumber military casualties. This means when wars are fought, average people who are just trying to live their lives and have no control over the actions of their government suffer the most harm. Families are torn apart, people are displaced, homes and cities are destroyed—some populations never recover from war.

4. There are usually no consequences for government officials who lie to get their country into a war or who cause harm to civilians through their actions. They pay no price for causing death, despair, and disability.

The Gulf of Tonkin Mystery

A declassified review of evidence by the National Security Administration Historian

Published in the NSA's classified journal in 2001

For the first time ever, what will be presented in the following narrative is the complete SIGINT [signals intelligence] version of what happened in the Gulf of Tonkin between 2 and 4 August 1964. Until now, the NSA has officially maintained that the second incident of 4 August occurred. This position was established in the initial SIGINT reports of 4 August and sustained through a series of summary reports issued shortly after the crisis. In October 1964, a classified chronology of events for 2 to 4 August in the Gulf of Tonkin was published by NSA which furthered the contention that the second attack had occurred.

In maintaining the official version of the attack, the NSA made use of surprisingly few published SIGINT reports - fifteen in all. The research behind the new version which follows is based on the discovery of an enormous amount of never-before-used SIGINT material. This included 122 relevant SIGINT products, along with watch center notes, oral history interviews, and messages among the various SIGINT and military command centers involved in the Gulf of Tonkin incidents. Naturally, this flood of new information changed dramatically the story of that night of 4/5 August. The most important element is that it is now known what the North Vietnamese Navy was doing that night. And with this information a nearly complete story finally can be told.

Two startling findings emerged from the new research. First, it is not simply that there is a different story as to what happened; it is that *no attack* happened that night. Through a compound of analytic errors and an unwillingness to consider contrary evidence, American SIGINT elements in the region and at NSA HQs reported Hanoi's plans to attack the two ships of the Desoto patrol. Further analytic errors and an obscuring of other information led to publication of more "evidence." In truth, Hanoi's navy was engaged in nothing that night but the salvage of two of the boats damaged on 2 August.

The second finding pertains to the handling of the SIGINT material related to the Gulf of Tonkin by individuals at NSA. Beginning with the period of the crisis in early August, into the days of the immediate aftermath, and continuing into October 1964, SIGINT information was presented in such a manner as to preclude responsible decisionmakers in the Johnson administration from having the complete and objective narrative of events of 4 August 1964. Instead, only SIGINT that supported the claim that the communists had attacked the two destroyers was given to administration officials.

The exact "how" and "why" for this effort to provide only the SIGINT that supported the claim of an attack remain unknown. There are no "smoking gun" memoranda or notes buried in the files that outline any plan or state a justification. Instead, the paper record speaks for itself on what happened... From this evidence, one can easily deduce the deliberate nature of these actions. And this observation makes sense, for there was a purpose to them: This was an active effort to make SIGINT fit the claim of what happened during the evening of 4 August in the Gulf of Tonkin.

Operation
SEA-SPRAY

Unbeknownst to the public, a series of covert experiments unfolded, shrouded in secrecy. From infections to subway tests, hidden truths gradually emerge, inviting inquiry into a concealed history.

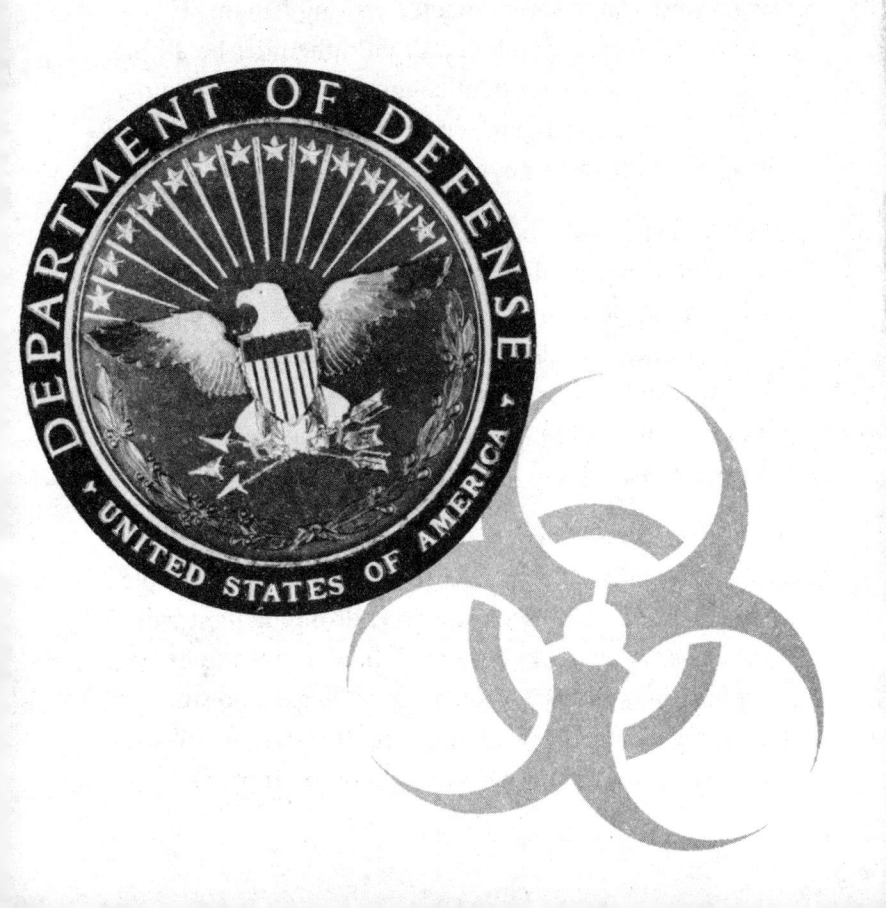

In October 1950, eleven people in the San Francisco Bay Area became suddenly and violently ill with severe urinary tract infections. Over the course of the next several months, drug rehabilitation facilities noted strange infections around the injection sites of intravenous drug users who were seeking treatment in their programs. One person even died. Doctors noted that all the patients had urine that was tinted slightly red but couldn't figure out what would have caused it. Since San Francisco is a large city, eleven people and some drug addicts exhibiting similar ailments didn't cause too much concern, so doctors shrugged it off as nothing more than a strange coincidence.

Two months later, several people visiting Panama City and Key West, Florida, developed slight difficulties breathing, itchy throats, and persistent coughs. None of the symptoms were bad enough to require medical care, so they just shrugged it off and enjoyed their trip.

There didn't seem to be any reason for this increase in seemingly random illnesses, leading many people to think that advancements in diagnosing methods, as well as better-educated doctors, was the explanation. It wasn't that there was suddenly *more* disease, authorities thought—it was just that doctors were getting better at finding disease that previously would have been missed.

Several years later, police in New York City received several phone calls over the course of five days from people who claimed to have seen someone dropping light bulbs onto the subway tracks at several different terminals. Since dropping light bulbs isn't technically illegal, and since police in New York City are usually pretty busy, no one ever followed up on the mysterious light bulb droppers.

Random infections, sniffles and coughs on vacations, and subway light bulb drops were, of course, totally unrelated to one another. Or were they?

Things Aren't Always What They Seem

After World War II, world governments began to consider the very real risks of biological agents—bacteria and viruses—being weaponized and used to inflict mass casualties on large civilian populations. They may have recognized that with each war, new and terrible ways of killing are discovered, and, unfortunately, there are always governments or groups willing to use them to shape the world in the image they imagine as ideal. Seeing the horrors of the Nazi death camps was perhaps a wake-up call to the world. People saw just how much darkness and depravity existed in the hearts of some people and the terrifying lengths they were willing to go to realize their plans.

Dark threats loomed large in the minds of those charged with protecting the citizens of the United States from ambush and annihilation. The military, in partnership with secret government agencies, set out to see just how easy it could be for an enemy to use biological weapons on US soil and how far-reaching the effects would be if they succeeded.

They embarked on a decades-long series of tests stretching from San Francisco to Key West to New York City—covering American cities in bacteria and chemicals without the knowledge or consent of those affected, and without any way to know if their tests would harm the unwitting participants.

In San Francisco, the US Navy conducted Operation Sea-Spray. The objective was to determine whether or not the United States was susceptible to a biological attack launched from the sea off the coast of the US mainland. A bacterium called *Serratia marcescens*, which is capable of living in both water and soil for long periods of time and produces a bright red pigment, was sprayed from US Navy ships along the Northern California coast. So was another, *Bacillus globigii*.

The US Navy wanted to see if the bacteria would enter the water systems of the Bay Area. The experiment was a success. The bacteria did make its way into the water system where it circulated long enough for the US Navy to conduct tests and determine that they had indeed discovered a vulnerability and a likely avenue of attack.

Although it was assumed that *Serratia marcescens* was harmless to humans, a week after the test began, eleven people suffered severe urinary tract infections. No connection to the experiments was made at the time, and no one was ever held accountable, even though one person died.

The bacteria were also dispersed across the other side of the continent in Key West and Panama City, Florida. Many people reported coughs, urinary tract infections, and respiratory irritation, but because no one knew that testing was being conducted, no one thought the sniffles and coughs were related.

A substance called *zinc cadmium sulfide*, which was once thought to be harmless but was later found to cause cancer, was sprayed in the atmosphere over America's Midwest. The airborne toxin traveled so far, so fast, that it was found as far east as New York.

And the light bulb subway incidents? Yes, that was the government too. For five days, covert operatives dropped light bulbs full of *Bacillus subtilis* onto subway tracks and down vents to measure how quickly it would become airborne and how long it would stay in the subways. By all estimates, the New York City subway system is still heavily contaminated with the bacteria from the original tests.

Cui Bono?

Medical and scientific experiments are necessary to advance us from where we are to our future potential. It takes lifesaving procedures from theory to practice and improves the quality of all of our lives. As vital as experiments and testing are, there is another essential component that sometimes gets overlooked: consent.

Consent to medical or scientific testing can be a tricky thing. Not many people are willing to sign themselves up to be guinea pigs in an experiment that could be potentially harmful—or even deadly. Likewise, testing new drugs, new medical procedures, and new therapies can be dangerous and can often end up causing more harm than good. Doctors and scientists sometimes find themselves in the frustrating situation of having a really good idea or a really promising procedure or product, but lacking any willing participants for the next phase of testing and development.

Good doctors and ethical scientists—people who respect bodily autonomy, the sanctity of human life, and human choice—often put research on hold until they are able to gather enough willing participants to conduct the necessary research. But not all doctors are good, and not all scientists are ethical. For those people, a lack of willing participants in research experiments doesn't mean they have to wait; to them it means they need to find a way around the moral or ethical problems standing in their way.

Sometimes, groups of researchers sidestep ethical roadblocks because they believe their research is uniquely important and, therefore, exempt from rules that apply to other researchers. Some of these more aggressive researchers work for the government, and are tasked with conceiving of every possible thing that a bad guy might do to cause harm to the citizens of their country, and then trying to figure out how that harm could come, and how they can stop it from happening. Although it is good to have a government and military that wants to take proactive steps to protect people, they often justify harming the very people they're supposed to protect in order to *hopefully* protect more people *later*.

Why Does This Matter?

No one should be subjected to experimental medical testing without their prior knowledge and consent. People should be able to safely and happily go about their lives—riding the subway, going to the beach, walking their dog, or playing with their children at the park—without having to fear that their government is spraying them with bacteria or chemicals that could potentially make them sick.

It seems pretty silly to even have to think about that because it's so obvious that it is wrong to test anything on people without consent. But examples of these types of tests are so numerous—for example, between 1949 and 1969 the US

Army conducted open-air tests using biological agents *239 times*—that one might wonder if the government operates under the same moral code as most of the rest of us… or if they operate under any moral code at all!

One of the important questions to ask when you discover that someone in power has done something sneaky and terrible is, "If they did *this*, and only stopped because they got caught, *what else* have they done, and what else would they do if they thought they could get away with it?" It is responsible to ask questions like this and to look at those in positions of power with skepticism.

What We Learned

1. US and foreign governments have conducted secret experiments with live bacteria and cancer-causing agents on their own civilian populations, causing harm and even death to people who unknowingly interacted with the chemicals or bacteria.

2. When governments say they will stop performing unethical experiments, there is no way to know if they actually do—the people are left to trust the very government that has already deceived and harmed them.

3. None of the people who thought up these experiments or carried them out have been punished for the harm they caused.

4. Technological advances since the 1950s would make it very easy for experimentation to take place on civilian populations without their knowledge or consent.

Biological Testing Involving Human Subjects by the Dept. of Defense

Excerpts from testimony to the US Senate Subcommittee on Health and Scientific Research

March 8, 1977

Colonel Carruth, U.S. Army, Chemical and Nuclear Biological Chemical Defense Division: The records indicate that there were 19 tests. Nineteen tests conducted in public domain using biological simulants. I will make a distinction, Senator, between biological simulants and nonbiological materials, for instance particles and other materials which were released to check dispersion patterns, but were not living materials. There were 27 of those tests conducted in the public domain.

Sen. Schweiker: Using which simulant?

Col. Carruth: *Serratia marcescens.*

Sen. Kennedy: Let us review the basic issue that we are talking about here, and that is simulant tests conducted in the public areas. That is what we are talking about here, are we not?

Col. Carruth: The majority of the simulant tests were conducted on military installations.

Sen. Kennedy: We are not talking about the military installations, we are talking about public domain in those areas. How many did you say were conducted?

Col. Carruth: Nineteen, sir.

Sen. Kennedy: Maybe you could just sort of describe the procedures a little bit to the best of your knowledge, and how they were collected and what actually happened in these areas, what you were trying to deal with?

Col. Carruth: The early tests that were conducted were specifically designed to determine the vulnerability. The initial tests conducted and listed in the report were ones in Washington, and these were to test the vulnerability of the Pentagon to simulated biological attacks.

They were testing to determine whether or not it could be done covertly, thereby infecting the members of the military services and knocking out our headquarters.

The next test that was conducted was one to determine the vulnerability of our Navy ships at sea to a biological attack. A test in San Francisco was to determine whether or not an enemy could conduct a biological attack at sea and infect the population of our cities.

I might say that with the simulants used, and the San Francisco test was done in 1950, the evidence that was available at that time indicated that both simulants, both *Serratia marcenscens* and *Bacillus globigii*, were nonpathogenic. Since they were simulants, we did not expect to find any effect on the human population.

Sen. Kennedy: I do not think that there is any question in the minds of the American people that open air testing is basically repugnant to our American system; that in many instances, at least some important instances, tests were conducted in the public domain...

ELECTRO SHOCK
HIGH VOLTAGE
What's happening? Who am I?
Interesting results... let's experiment with more drugs!

Project MK-ULTRA

Unseen forces harnessed the power of the mind, conducting covert experiments that twisted reality. But have the echoes of these mind-altering endeavors truly faded, or do they persist today?

PROJECT MKULTRA, THE CIA'S PROGRAM OF RESEARCH IN BEHAVIORAL MODIFICATION

JOINT HEARING
BEFORE THE
SELECT COMMITTEE ON INTELLIGENCE
AND THE
SUBCOMMITTEE ON
HEALTH AND SCIENTIFIC RESEARCH
OF THE
COMMITTEE ON HUMAN RESOURCES
UNITED STATES SENATE
NINETY-FIFTH CONGRESS
FIRST SESSION

AUGUST 3, 1977

On April 10, 1953, Allen Dulles rose to a podium to deliver a shocking address to the assembled alumni of his alma mater, Princeton University, at a conference in Hot Springs, Virginia.

The Korean War was just about to conclude, creating a new Communist North Korea. Joseph Stalin, the dictator who ruled the Soviet Union, had died a month prior. Dwight D. Eisenhower, the famed Army general, had just become president of the United States, taking office in January. He and countless Americans saw the Soviet Union as a major threat whose communist ideas needed to be contained and defeated.

Dulles was the first civilian director of the CIA and had taken office—appointed by Eisenhower—on February 26. Now, several weeks later, he warned his audience, and the American people more broadly, about a new "mind control" program being conducted by the Soviets. "Its aim," he said, "is to condition the mind so that it no longer reacts on a free will or rational basis but responds to impulses implanted from outside." He continued:

> If we are to counter this kind of warfare we must understand the techniques the Soviet is adopting to control men's minds...
>
> The human mind is the most delicate of all instruments. It is so finely adjusted, so susceptible to the impact of outside influences that it is proving a malleable tool in the hands of sinister men... We in the West are somewhat handicapped in brain warfare.

Dulles further claimed that "it is hard for us to realize that in the great area behind the Iron Curtain a vast experiment is underway to change men's minds, working on them continuously from youth to old age."

As you might imagine, the audience was alarmed to hear this revelation from the director of the CIA. More and more Americans became concerned with the power and influence of the Soviet Union and the nefarious schemes they were conducting such as this mind control business.

Things Aren't Always What They Seem

Three days after giving this speech, Dulles secretly ordered his spy agency to enter the mind control business as well. So much for being "somewhat handicapped," right?

Known as Project MK-Ultra, this top-secret government program involved mind control experiments using drugs, electroshock therapy, toxins, hypnosis, radiation, and more. Some participants had volunteered freely for the program, but most were enrolled under coercion or without any knowledge that they were human guinea pigs for the CIA's activities.

Soldiers, prisoners, mentally impaired individuals, and other vulnerable members of society were lab rats for Dulles's project. While governments had long sought to engineer consent through changing popular opinion, now ours was turning to weaponizing science and psychology to coerce consent by reengineering the human brain. Dulles attacked the "sinister men" in the Soviet Union for doing this. Now he was directly overseeing mind control experiments at levels that would dwarf anything being done by the Soviets.

Even worse, those carrying out this vast experiment concluded that "unwitting [participants] would be desirable." For over a decade, MK-Ultra involved 149 projects using drug experimentation and other tactics, often on unsuspecting individuals.

To avoid scrutiny, the CIA set up secret detention facilities in areas under American control, such as in Japan, Germany, and the Philippines, so that they could avoid criminal prosecution if they were discovered. CIA officers captured people suspected of being "enemy agents" and other people they felt were "expendable" and began experimenting on and torturing them. These prisoners were interrogated while being given drugs, shocked with electricity, and subjected to extremes of temperature and sensory isolation.

Where was the oversight? Obviously, a secretive CIA program would not come to public light, but one would hope that the inspector general—a role designed to identify and stop fraud and abuse—would have urged restraint and compliance with the law. In this case, quite the opposite happened. A 1963 report from the CIA's inspector general says this:

> Precautions must be taken not only to protect operations from exposure to enemy forces but also to conceal these activities from the American public in general. The knowledge that the [CIA] is engaging in unethical and illicit activities would have serious repercussions in political and diplomatic circles and would be detrimental to the accomplishment of its mission.

The American public first learned of this conspiracy two decades after it started, in 1975, when a congressional committee issued a report detailing some aspects of MK-Ultra's programs. Much of what these elected officials learned and revealed came from the inspector general's report, which survived the CIA director's 1973 order to destroy all files connected to Project MK-Ultra. The report had been incorrectly stored in another building, surviving the purge and preserving information about this vast conspiracy conducted on countless individuals.

Cui Bono?

Dulles had warned that others' efforts to control men's minds have "such far reaching implications that it is high time for us to realize what it means and the problems it presents in thwarting our own program for spreading the gospel of freedom." But do government officials truly care about spreading the so-called "gospel of freedom?"

Dulles was not wrong—the Soviets were indeed operating mind control experiments. Many governments were. The CIA believed that China and North Korea were also operating such programs. The Nazis had done it, with doctors experimenting on prisoners at Auschwitz and Dachau. The CIA recruited many of these individuals after World War II to continue their work, now (theoretically) in support of those promoting "freedom."

Not all of these researchers were in on the conspiracy. In some cases, scientists were given grants to fund their work, provided by CIA front organizations. In these situations, scientists either did not know that the CIA was using their work for these purposes, or at least they had plausible deniability to shield them from future legal consequences. In any case, the patients did not consent to the testing.

Americans were right to be concerned about the Soviets and other Communists trying to manipulate people. And government officials who wanted to find ways to more easily thwart Communist efforts had reasonable intentions. But the ends don't justify the means—having good intentions of stopping evil Communists doesn't mean it's okay to become evil yourself, experimenting on unsuspecting people.

Why Does This Matter?

Governments have long used propaganda to persuade their citizens to support what leaders propose. These tactics are used to encourage support for a war, an election campaign, a bailout program, a pandemic response, and a host of other situations. The father of modern propaganda, Edward Bernays, once said, "The engineering of consent is the very essence of the democratic process, the freedom to persuade and suggest."

The methods used by Project MK-Ultra represent a far more sophisticated and nefarious approach to the "engineering of consent." Where propaganda typically relies on the written or spoken word to plant ideas in a person's mind, the CIA's conspiratorial mind control program sought ways to use chemical and behavioral modification to alter a person's perceptions and actions.

Of course, those involved had a way to soothe their conscience—after all, they were simply trying to catch up to the Soviets and make sure that their mind control activities could be thwarted and overpowered. But that's the thing—evil deeds always have excuses. There's always a boogeyman to vanquish or emergency to stop. There's always a reason for those in power to try and get *more* power. We can't do bad things in the name of creating good.

What little information about Project MK-Ultra that survived the CIA's destruction of evidence was revealed to the American people, showing the hypocrisy of Dulles's warning in 1953. But it raises a question: if a secretive government agency could conspire like this over half a century ago, and with the advances in technology today, is it silly to think that similar programs aren't happening now?

What We Learned

1. Government officials pointed to an enemy's activities to raise Americans' concern and increase their opposition to their efforts, while doing the exact same thing themselves.

2. The CIA went to great lengths to make sure the public didn't learn about their actions, going so far as to destroy nearly all records that showed what they were up to.

3. To avoid oversight and criminal consequences, the CIA conducted many of their activities overseas on people from other countries.

4. The inspector general, instead of putting a stop to this abuse of power, helped conceal it from the public and encouraged continued secrecy of the program.

5. Nobody was fired or criminally prosecuted for their involvement in Project MK-Ultra.

An MK-Ultra Document

Published in 1977 by the Select Committee on Intelligence of the United States Congress

May 5, 1955

A portion of the Research and Development Program of TSS/Chemical Division is devoted to the discovery of the following materials and methods:

1. Substances which will promote illogical thinking and impulsiveness to the point where the recipient would be discredited in public.

2. Substances which increase the efficiency of mentation and perception.

3. Materials which will prevent or counteract the intoxicating effect of alcohol.

4. Materials which will promote the intoxicating effect of alcohol.

5. Materials which will produce the signs and symptoms of recognized diseases in a reversible way so they may be used for malingering, etc.

6. Materials which will render the induction of hypnosis easier or otherwise enhance its usefulness.

7. Substances which will enhance the ability of individuals to withstand privation, torture, and coercion during interrogation and so-called "brain-washing".

8. Materials and physical methods which will produce amnesia for events preceding and during their use.

9. Physical methods of producing shock and confusion over extended periods of time and capable of surreptitious use.

10. Substances which produce physical disablement such as paralysis of the legs, acute anemia, etc.

11. Substances which will produce "pure" euphoria with no subsequent let-down.

12. Substances which alter personality structure in such a way the tendency of the recipient to become dependent upon another person is enhanced.

13. A material which will cause mental confusion of such a type the individual under its influence will find it difficult to maintain a fabrication under questioning.

14. Substances which will lower the ambition and general working efficiency of men when administered in undetectable amounts.

15. Substances which promote weakness or distortion of the eyesight or hearing faculties, preferably without permanent effects.

16. A knockout pill which can be surreptitiously administered in drinks, food, cigarettes, as an aerosol, etc., which will be safe to use, provide a maximum of amnesia, and be suitable for use by agent types on an ad hoc basis.

17. A material which can be surreptitiously administered by the above routes and which in very small amounts will make it impossible for a person to perform physical activity.

The
TUSKEGEE
Experiment

A covert medical study exploited vulnerable individuals, denying them treatment and perpetuating their suffering. Unveiling the hidden horrors of unethical research, it raises profound concerns about the price paid for scientific progress.

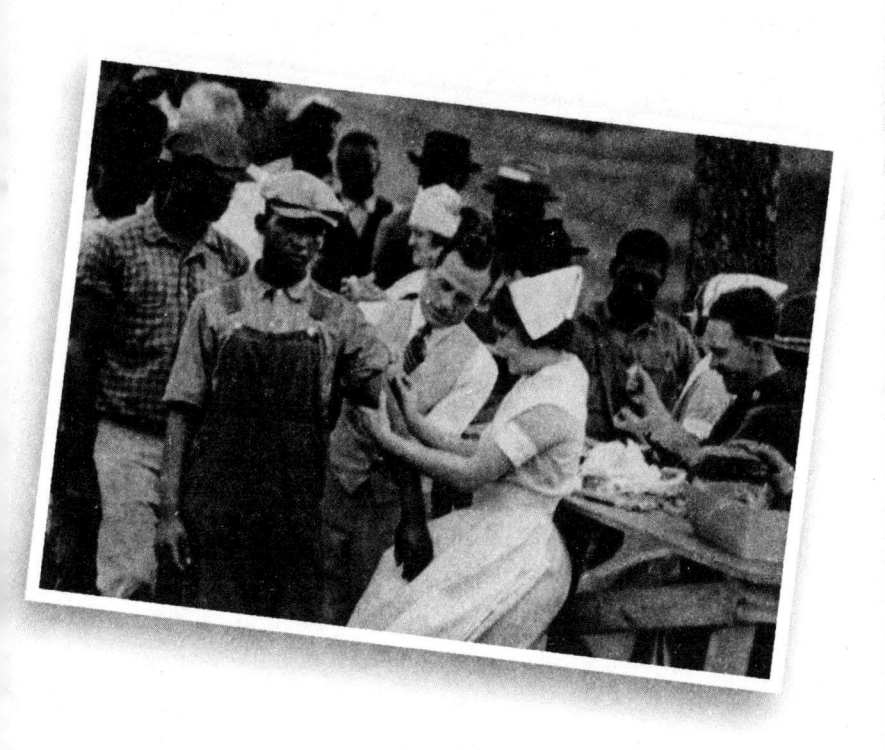

In the 1930s, a condition called *bad blood* plagued men in rural Alabama. They would develop rashes and experience fatigue and painful joints. While the disease was fairly widespread, those without access to medical care—mostly poor sharecroppers in Black communities—seemed to be suffering the most.

In response, the government deployed doctors to provide aid to a group of six hundred men. The doctors ran much-needed medical tests, diagnosed their conditions, and gave them treatments to help ease their symptoms while research was conducted in the hopes of someday discovering a cure.

Despite the government doctors trying their best, some of the men eventually died since a successful treatment was not made available to them.

Things Aren't Always What They Seem

Except… the government didn't help. Instead, they caused the problem.

In 1932, in partnership with the Tuskegee Institute, government officials began a study to learn the effects of untreated syphilis on the human body. It was first called the "Tuskegee Study of Untreated Syphilis in the Negro Male" and involved 600 Black men—399 with syphilis and 201 who did not have the supposed disease. The men were told that they were being treated for "bad blood," a term used back then when doctors didn't really know what was wrong or when someone was unwell but too poor to be seen by a professional. What was called "bad blood" was in reality something like syphilis, anemia, or fatigue. The men believed they were part of a program that offered free medical care to poor people in rural areas, and as part of their enrollment they received free medical exams, regular medical "treatment," and free meals. They were also given burial insurance which would help their families pay for the cost of a funeral should they die.

The government originally planned to run the experiment for six months, but the program was extended each time it was nearing its proposed end. The men being studied didn't know that they were test subjects in an experiment. They never consented to be studied—they always thought they were receiving free medical care.

Eleven years into the experiment, penicillin was widely used to treat syphilis, but none of the "patients" in the Tuskegee Study were given the lifesaving drug. Instead, researchers pressured local doctors to not treat any of the men in the study. They didn't want the results to be influenced by treatment of the sick men. Remember, the experiment aimed to find out what would happen to someone who had *untreated* syphilis—basically someone who had the disease *forever*.

In 1972, the Associated Press broke a story that leaked some information about the Tuskegee Experiment. As a result, an advisory panel was appointed by the Department of Health and Scientific Affairs to determine whether the study should be halted. The panel found that the experiment was, "ethically unjustified," and that the "results were disproportionately meager compared to the known risks to human subjects involved." Later that year, the program was officially shut down.

In all, twenty-eight men died while under the "care" of these doctors and scientists. Hundreds more died due to related complications. More than a hundred others were left permanently disabled, and many of their wives and children were also infected. In 1975, the government, in an attempt to make things right, finally began providing treatment for the sick men and healthcare and medical benefits to the wives and children of those whose lives they had ruined by withholding treatment in the name of research.

Cui Bono?

The Tuskegee experiment began over a decade before a treatment for syphilis was known. The doctors who conducted the experiment reasoned that since there was no known treatment, it would be okay to observe a group of people and hopefully discover more about the effects of the disease over a period of time. Researchers have often used this method when learning about an illness for which there is no cure, except usually the participants in the study know that they are part of a research experiment and have given their consent to be studied.

In this case, the researchers gave themselves permission to study people who didn't know they were being studied and who thought they were being treated for an illness. Those who conducted the experiment eventually convinced themselves that the things they learned about syphilis could be used to help other people and decided that the lives of the people in their study were worth trading for the lives of other people later. Even after a treatment for syphilis was discovered, the research team opted to allow their unknowing test subjects to suffer severe disability and death so that they could more fully observe all the possible outcomes of an untreated infection.

The benefit to science and medicine was nominal. It was learned that syphilis could cause a variety of physical and psychological ailments, be passed on to others—even newborn babies—and eventually could cause death. Of course, when treated with penicillin, none of these terrible things happened, which means most of the people who suffered and died in Tuskegee could have quickly recovered and lived full, healthy lives.

But even if they had made great medical discoveries that resulted in treatments that would save the lives of thousands, would it have been right to sacrifice the lives of these six hundred men and their families?

Why Does This Matter?

The Tuskegee experiment was conducted on real people who thought they were receiving medical care. They were targeted because they were poor and unwell, and doctors in the surrounding areas agreed not to offer treatment or care because it could disrupt the study. The experiment lasted for forty years and continued for nearly thirty years beyond the discovery of a cure for syphilis. During those years, women and children became infected with the disease and suffered terribly without any relief and without any actual medical care. The US government lied to vulnerable people, withheld treatment that could have cured them, allowed them to pass their sickness on to others, allowed those people to suffer, and allowed many of their test subjects to actually die, all in the name of "medical research."

The program only stopped when someone who knew what was happening spoke out. Later, it was discovered that the US government had funded a similar program in Guatemala with similar methods and similar results.

The people who conducted these experiments were not punished—the government simply said, "Sorry we did that to you," wrote a few checks and moved on to something else. There was no justice for the many victims.

If someone does something terrible to another person, only stops because they got caught, and then suffers no consequence for the harm they caused, are they likely to stop doing terrible things to other people? Probably not. They will likely continue doing terrible things with the knowledge that nothing will happen to them, even if they get caught. There is always medical research that needs to be conducted, and there are always poor, vulnerable, sick people who are likely to trust someone from the government who is offering to help them for free.

What We Learned

1. The US government told people that they were providing them with free healthcare, but they were actually performing experiments on them.

2. In the name of science, people with treatable diseases were deprived of the medicine they needed to regain health. The diseases were allowed to be passed on to

the families of those being experimented on, and the test subjects were allowed to suffer and die.

3. Often, when something the government is secretly doing is exposed, other (sometimes worse) secrets come to light as well.

4. People typically trust their doctor to help them maintain or regain health, but the government has the power to pressure or persuade some doctors to violate their oath and allow their patients to be harmed in order to further some alleged greater goal of research.

5. Secret tests and experiments run by the government are likely to continue until someone who knows what is happening speaks out.

Investigative Report

By the Tuskegee Syphilis Study Ad Hoc Advisory Panel for the US Dept. of Health, Education, and Welfare

April 24, 1973

The Tuskegee Study was one of several investigations that were taking place in the 1930s with the ultimate objective of venereal disease control in the United States. Beginning in 1926, the United States Public Health Service, with the cooperation of other organizations, actively engaged in venereal disease control work.

In 1929, the United States Public Health Service entered into a cooperative demonstration study with the Julius Rosenwald Fund and state and local departments of health in the control of venereal disease in six southern states: Mississippi (Bolivar County); Tennessee (Tipton County); Georgia (Glynn County); Alabama (Macon County); North Carolina (Pitt County); Virginia (Albermarle County). These syphilis control demonstrations took place from 1930-1932 and disclosed a high prevalence of syphilis (35%) in the Macon County survey. Macon County was 82.4% Negro. The cultural status of this Negro population was low and the illiteracy rate was high.

1. There is no protocol which documents the original intent of the study. None of the literature searches or interviews with participants in the study gave any evidence that a written protocol ever existed for this study.

2. There is no evidence that informed consent was gained from the human participants in this study. Such consent would and should have included knowledge of the risk of

human life for the involved parties and information re: possible infections of innocent, nonparticipating parties such as friends and relatives.

3. In 1932, there was a known risk to human life and transmission of the disease in latent and late syphilis was believed to be possible.

4. The study as announced and continually described as involving "untreated" male Negro subjects was not a study of "untreated" subjects.

5. There is evidence that control subjects who became syphilitic were transferred to the "untreated" group.

6. In the absence of a definitive protocol, there is no evidence or assurance that standardization of evaluative procedures, which are essential to the validity and reliability of a scientific study, existed at any time. This fact leaves open to question the true scientific merits of a longitudinal study of this nature.

In retrospect, the Public Health Service Study of Untreated Syphilis in the Male Negro in Macon County, Alabama, was ethically unjustified in 1932. This judgment made in 1973 about the conduct of the study in 1932 is made with the advantage of hindsight acutely sharpened over some forty years, concerning an activity in a different age with different social standards. Nevertheless one fundamental ethical rule is that a person should not be subjected to avoidable risk of death or physical harm unless he freely and intelligently consents. There is no evidence that such consent was obtained from the participants in this study.

We've sold thousands of military-grade weapons to the Mexican cartels. Now we'll track those weapons back to their bosses.
Brilliant! How will you track the weapons?
Hmm... I haven't yet thought that far ahead.
This plan is so bad it just might work.
United States
Mexico

Operation FAST & FURIOUS

A risky operation to track criminals instead leads to unintended consequences when weapons fall into the wrong hands.

NEWS
BORDER PATROL AGENT, BRIAN TERRY KILLED

In the early 2000s, a new trend emerged in Hollywood. Filmmakers, in an effort to break from the norm, began producing movies without happy endings. Sometimes, the bad guys were even painted as the good guys, or at least as *kind of* good—with complicated reasons for doing bad things that made the audience view them if not with favor, at least with a little bit of sympathy.

Some of the movies were instant hits as people embraced a different way of viewing the complications of life and personal relationships. But some were just so terrible, the plots so unbelievable, and the villains so bad, there was no way any audience could learn to love them—they were bound to flop. Take this plot for example:

Set in the American Southwest, the war on drugs serves as the backdrop for the story. Warring cartels are wreaking havoc all across Mexico, and their violence and debauchery is spilling over the border into the US. No one seems to be able to stop the flow of drugs and criminals, and no one can come up with any new ideas that show any promise of being successful. Finally, a dimwitted federal agent gets what he thinks is a brilliant idea.

"What if," he proposes, "we actually *give* weapons to the bad guys?" He goes on to explain that he's certain the cartels can be infiltrated and the big players brought down if gun shops across Texas and Arizona allow known drug dealers and criminals to buy guns. He recognizes that this is in stark contrast to the current method of keeping guns *out* of the hands of criminals and drug dealers, but he theorizes that low-level criminals will lead them right to the bigger criminals. The serial numbers on the guns will make all of this easily traceable. The cartels, he figures, will be busted by Christmas.

Reluctantly, he gets permission to put his plan into action. After all, they've tried everything else, and nothing seems to be working. What could it hurt?

The movie plays out about how you'd suspect. The bad guys use the guns to do bad things. The federal agents bumble around the US and Mexico trying to keep track of the guns but ultimately fail to trace most of them. The ones they do get their hands on are usually collected as evidence at crime scenes where they've been used to kill innocent people.

The film flops (of course), and the people who made it get shamed out of town and have to take jobs teaching stage acting at the local community college. The end.

Things Aren't Always What They Seem

It's actually worse than you think—because this wasn't the plot to a terrible movie. These were real events that actually happened with the full backing of the US government, and the people responsible weren't shamed out of town.

In 2010, the US Bureau of Alcohol, Tobacco, and Firearms (ATF) initiated a program that became known as Operation Fast and Furious. (You can tell they were very serious and thoughtful people because they named their operation after a movie franchise about hot rods.) Their plan was to allow "suspicious individuals" to purchase guns and then follow these individuals. When they went to hand off those guns to the Mexican cartel, everyone involved would be arrested and charged, and the ATF would recover the guns. They were sure it was a foolproof plan.

Instead, the ATF basically just sold a bunch of guns (about two thousand) to the Mexican drug cartels. They found that it was nearly impossible to trace the guns once they were in the hands of the bad guys, and the guns they did find and recover were usually left at crime scenes.

Some good ATF agents knew that what the agency was doing was wrong, causing harm to innocent people, and betraying the trust of Americans—particularly those living along the southern border who were being victimized by cartel violence. The agents' concerns were ignored, and Fast and Furious continued.

The program probably would have continued, hidden from the American public and from any accountability, had a US Border Control agent not been killed in a shootout between armed robbers and drug smugglers at the Arizona border in December 2010. As his death was investigated, authorities discovered that the agent had been shot with one of the guns allowed to walk into the hands of the cartels by the ATF.

Through its attempt to do a few bad things in order to keep potentially worse bad things from happening, the US government actually became an arms dealer for the Mexican drug cartels.

Cui Bono?

The ATF said they allowed criminals and suspected (and known) drug dealers to buy guns, so they could track them and then catch bigger criminals and drug dealers at some later date. It was pretty easy to see all the ways their plan could go wrong, but they proceeded anyway, and sure enough, their plan went very wrong.

Far from bringing down the cartels, putting criminals in prison, and shutting off the supply of drugs flowing across the Mexican border into the United States, Fast and Furious really just supplied guns to criminals, who used them to kill innocent people. Most of the guns disappeared and are assumed to still be in the hands of violent criminals in both Mexico and the United States.

The ATF probably would have liked to have swept this operation under the rug—it was an embarrassment to the government and caused a stain on Barack Obama's presidency. It also caused a lot of ATF agents to lose faith in their organization. They knew putting guns in the hands of bad guys was not the right thing to do, no matter how much their bosses said it would pay off later.

In the end, the ATF lost, the government lost, the American and Mexican people lost, and the drug dealers and criminals won.

Why Does This Matter?

Operation Fast and Furious is an example of a fairly recent government scandal. Most examples of government conspiracies and misdeeds seem to have taken place a long time ago—back in the 1950s and 1960s when the threats of communism and nuclear war affected every decision that government and military leaders made. It's easy to look at these stories and think that government agencies lying to their citizens, putting them in harm's way in the name of the "greater good," or letting bad guys get away with their crimes was something from a different time—a bygone era—and that we have a better system in place now that keeps the government and its agencies in check and accountable to the people.

But that isn't true. It only seems like all the bad stuff happened a long time ago because it usually takes decades for curious and persistent journalists to gain access to classified information or for whistleblowers to gather the courage to come forward. Operation Fast and Furious teaches us that government agencies are still very much acting in the same way they always have. They are putting plans into action that they think, maybe someday, could benefit the country without caring how many people are likely to be harmed along the way or how badly their scheme could go wrong.

What Can We Learn?

1. Government agencies can plan and implement operations that enable criminals and cause harm to innocent people and then suffer no consequences when their plans fail.

2. Gun laws, although strict for law-abiding citizens, can be broken or bent in the name of allowing criminals to access them in the hopes of catching bigger, and worse,

criminals later.

3. The government will enact programs and policies that have the potential to cause loss of life or harm to innocent people if they think that a greater good can be achieved in the future.

4. The consequences of failed programs and policies persist long after the program has ended. Those who were responsible for it have moved on, been promoted, or retired.

A Review of ATF's Operation Fast and Furious

Office of the Inspector General,
Oversight and Review Division

September 2012

On October 31, 2009, special agents working in the Phoenix office of the Bureau of Alcohol, Tobacco, Firearms and Explosives (ATF) received information from a local gun store about the recent purchases of multiple AK47 style rifles by four individuals. Agents began investigating the purchases and soon came to believe that the men were so-called "straw purchasers" involved in a large-scale gun trafficking organization responsible for buying guns for transport to violent Mexican drug trafficking organizations. This investigation was later named "Operation Fast and Furious."

By the time ATF and the U.S. Attorney's Office for the District of Arizona (U.S. Attorney's Office) publicly announced the indictment in the case on January 25, 2011, agents had identified more than 40 subjects believed to be connected to a trafficking conspiracy responsible for purchasing over 2,000 firearms for approximately $1.5 million in cash. The vast majority of the firearms purchased by Operation Fast and Furious subjects were AK-47 style rifles and FN Herstal 5.7 caliber pistols. During the course of the investigation, ATF agents seized only about 100 of the firearms purchased, the result of a strategy jointly pursued by ATF and the U.S. Attorney's Office that deferred taking overt enforcement action against the individual straw purchasers while seeking to build a case against the leaders of the organization.

Numerous firearms bought by straw purchasers were later recovered by law enforcement officials at crime scenes in Mexico and the United States. One such recovery occurred in connection with the tragic shooting death of a federal law enforcement agent, U.S. Customs and Border Protection Agent Brian Terry.

On January 16, 2010, one of the straw purchasers, Jaime Avila, purchased three AK-47 style rifles from a Phoenix-area gun store. ATF agents learned about that purchase 3 days later and, consistent with the investigative strategy in the case, made no effort to locate Avila or seize the rifles although ATF had identified Avila as a suspect in November 2009. Two of the three rifles purchased by Avila on January 16 were recovered 11 months later at the scene of the murder of Agent Terry, who was shot and killed on December 14, 2010, as he tried to arrest persons believed to be illegally entering the United States.

Although the Federal Bureau of Investigation (FBI) was assigned to investigate the murder of Agent Terry, the senior leadership of ATF and the Department of Justice (Department or DOJ) took little action in the immediate aftermath of Agent Terry's death to learn more about an ATF investigation that involved the trafficking of approximately 2,000 weapons over many months, and how guns purchased by a previously-identified subject of that investigation ended up being recovered at the scene of Agent Terry's murder.

The flaws in Operation Fast and Furious became widely publicized as a result of the willingness of a few ATF agents to publicly report what they knew about it, and the conduct of the investigation became the subject of a Congressional inquiry.

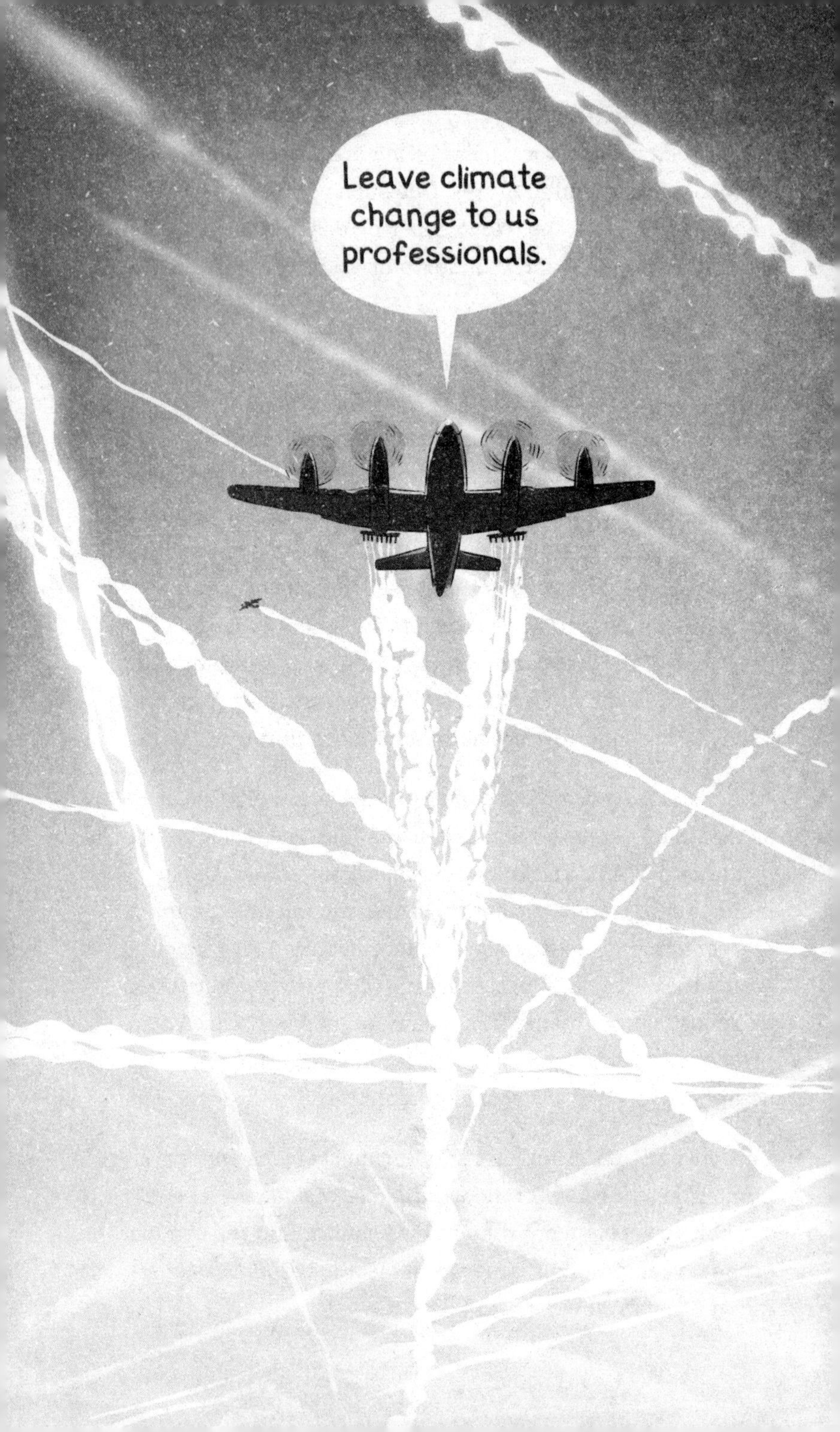
Leave climate change to us professionals.

Operation POPEYE

In the jungles of Vietnam, an enigmatic phenomenon unfolded—an unprecedented string of rainy seasons during a tumultuous period. Unbeknownst to many, there was more to these peculiar weather patterns than meets the eye.

Although it is always wet in the jungles of Vietnam, there were several years in late 1960s and early 1970s that were marked by unusual rainy seasons—periods of strange weather where clouds seemed to suddenly gather, fill with rain, and burst, drenching those beneath them.

The United States was in the midst of a war with North Vietnam. US troops had occasion to notice that the wet weather seemed to sometimes favor their operations. They would be having a difficult time stopping the Viet Cong from using a particular bridge or road to transport troops and supplies that they later used to stage attacks on US forces; then the rain would start, and within a couple of days the road had been washed away, or the bridge rendered impassable and damaged beyond repair.

While bridges and roads are vital for armies to win wars, there are other, less visible essentials as well. Someone raised on a farm probably would have noticed that the strange weather also hindered the North Vietnamese in another way. Farmers plant their crops at just the right time of year to ensure they will get the right amount of sun, rain, and warm or cool weather to mature into well-formed, usable food. But when weather becomes unpredictable—like when rainy seasons continue for much longer than usual or during periods of drought—crops often fail. They might wither and dry up from lack of water or turn yellow and wilted if the ground is too wet. The excessive rain caused many Vietnamese farmers to lose entire crops—food that was going to be used to supply the army (and the rest of Vietnam!) with much-needed food in the future.

Some American soldiers thought the strange weather was Providence—a sign that they were favored—that even

Mother Nature was conspiring to help them win the war. Some thought it was just good luck, and some cursed the constant rain and wished it would stop, welcoming a chance to finally dry out, even if the enemy got a break from the drizzle as well. Finally, about the time the last US plane headed for home, the weather resumed its natural cycle, and the soggy years came to an end.

Things Aren't Always What They Seem

Modern technology has given man (and governments) the ability to control things that have previously been out of their reach. Armies once had to march wherever they wanted to go; later, through technological advances, they were able to use chariots, then wagons and trains, trucks, tanks, and airplanes. Some battlefields are now reached remotely and the battles fought with drones! But the one thing all armies across all time have had to deal with was the weather. Weather impacts the good guys and the bad guys just the same—you can't control the weather.

Or *can* you?

In 1967, the United States military launched a top-secret operation known as Operation Popeye. The goal of the operation was to extend the monsoon season in areas of Laos and Vietnam that were vulnerable to seasonal flooding. To do this, planes flew through clouds and dropped silver iodide particles into the atmosphere that caused rainfall and disrupted normal air currents. Popeye was first proposed in 1966 by Dr. Leonard Sullivan, Assistant Director for Defense Research and Engineering. He came up with the idea after reading about how cloud seeding had been used to induce rainfall in arid regions of the United States. Sullivan believed that if cloud seeding could be used to cause rain, it could also be used to extend the monsoon season.

Sullivan's superior, Dr. John Foster, liked the proposal and got approval from Defense Secretary Robert McNamara for Popeye to go ahead. From 1967 to 1972, planes flew over Laos and Vietnam dropping silver iodide into the atmosphere. US military personnel carried out cloud-seeding missions using a converted C-130 transport plane. The crew would fly into an existing storm and then ignite the canisters of silver iodide to release particle-rich smoke and cause a reaction.

Popeye had a significant impact on the Vietnam War. Prior to the operation, Communist forces were able to freely move supplies and troops during the dry season. However, after Popeye began, they were forced to slow down due to heavy rains and flooding. This gave the United States an advantage in battle as they were able to launch surprise attacks on enemy forces. The military's goal with the program was to extend the monsoon season for thirty to forty-five days as well as increase the amount of rainfall during storms.

After reporters began publicizing what the government was doing, shining a light on the program and its impacts on the Vietnamese people, Popeye was eventually discontinued in 1972. No one was ever held responsible for the damage caused to the environment or the unethical nature of the project.

Despite the controversy surrounding Popeye, cloud seeding continues to be used for various purposes today. In fact, it is now commonly used by ski resorts in order to produce artificial snowfall, by event venues to guarantee sunny wedding days, and by farmers in order to increase crop yields.

Cui Bono?

The US military discovered that weather manipulation was actually possible, and they set their new technology to work to help them get the upper hand in their fight against the Viet Cong army. By extending the rainy season through cloud-seeding operations, the US was able to turn Mother Nature against their enemy. Bridges washed away, roads were impassable for weeks or months, and the enemy was cold, wet, and demoralized—looking at the sky wondering how much longer the rain could possibly fall.

But the earth has its cycles for a reason, and it turns out blocking the sun and causing constant rain impacts more than just roads, bridges and the morale of the enemy. Soon, crops began to fail—not just the crops of enemy fighters, but the crops of regular people who were just trying to survive as their country was ravaged by war. The drinking water was contaminated, illness spread, livestock died, and people began to worry that they wouldn't be able to feed their families or care for their children anymore.

Who decided that the people of Vietnam had to be the test subjects for the United States' new weather-control technology? Who had authority to make that decision, and was that person to be trusted to think about *all* the possible outcomes and consequences of their actions? Was there any accountability if what they did caused harm to innocent people? The truth is there was no accountability, and few people knew or cared that innocent people were suffering and dying in the never-ending storms artificially enhanced to win a war that ultimately couldn't be won.

Why Does This Matter?

The technology used to control and manipulate weather wasn't simply put away after the end of the Vietnam War. Although it was still in its early stages, it had proven to be a useful tool—one that could certainly be refined and expanded upon for future use.

The same is true for many technologies and products developed for war. They don't simply get placed on a shelf or stuck in a storage closet after they've served their purpose. Many technologies were first tested in war and later developed for everyday use and application. For example, the company that developed Agent Orange—a pesticide sprayed by US forces in Vietnam which caused millions of deaths and permanent disabilities in both the people of Vietnam and US service members—is now one of the biggest agricultural manufacturers in the world.

Monsanto develops seed technologies, and their pesticides and fertilizers are sprayed on nearly a quarter of all farmland in the world. They made a lot of their early money by selling the toxic Agent Orange to the US government and used the research done on human test subjects (the Vietnamese people and US troops) to develop later technologies.

As world leaders shift their focus to "climate change" and seek new ways to mitigate what they believe are the dangerous impacts of weather, it would be naive to forget that decades ago governments knew they could spray particles into the sky and cause the weather to do what they wanted it to. For example, in late 2022 it was revealed that the White House had begun implementing a five-year research program into "climate interventions" which included activities such as having planes spray reflective particles at very high altitudes to try and block incoming sunlight to slow down "climate change."

It is unlikely that powerful people who want to change the way we live have forgotten that weather-manipulation technology exists or that it has remained in storage since the end of the Vietnam War. Quite the opposite, really—such technology is still seen as viable by many today.

What We Learned

1. Technology that allows for the manipulation of weather has been available since at least the 1960s.

2. Government agencies, military leaders, and scientists will work together to meet their immediate goals without caring that the things they are doing impact everyone, including innocent people.

3. The government and media will conspire to disparage those who question what they see with their own eyes by labeling them "conspiracy theorists." This label discourages other people from questioning official narratives because they don't want to be likewise labeled.

Weather Modification in North Vietnam and Laos

Memorandum From the Deputy Under Secretary of State for Political Affairs to the Secretary of State

January 13, 1967

The Department of Defense has requested our approval to initiate the operational phase of Project Popeye in selected areas along the infiltration routes in North Vietnam and southern Laos. The objective of the program is to produce sufficient rainfall along these lines of communication to interdict or at least interfere with truck traffic between North and South Vietnam. Recently improved cloud seeding techniques would be applied on a sustained basis, in a non-publicized effort to induce continued rainfall through the months of the normal dry season.

A test phase of Project Popeye was approved by State and Defense and conducted during October 1966 in a strip of the Lao Panhandle generally east of the Bolovens Plateau in the valley of the Se Kong River. The test was conducted without consultation with Lao authorities (but with Ambassador Sullivan's knowledge and concurrence) and, to the best of our knowledge, remains unknown to other than a severely limited number of U.S. officials.

During the test phase, more than 50 cloud seeding experiments were conducted. The results are viewed by DOD as outstandingly successful.

In our view, the experiments were undeniably successful, indicating that, at least under weather and terrain conditions such as those involved, the U.S. Government has realized a capability of significant weather modification. If anything, the tests were "too successful"—neither the volume of induced rainfall nor the extent of area affected can be precisely predicted. The only absolute control, therefore, is after the fact, i.e., to halt cloud-seeding missions.

The present DOD proposal would grant authority for the conduct of cloud seeding activities on a sustained basis. For designated areas in North Vietnam, it would mean taking advantage of the present northeast monsoon (the "Crachin") to increase normal rainfall. The objective is to inhibit overland vehicular movement and to reinforce the bottlenecks already created at stream crossings by the bombing of bridges and ferry installations. With respect to Laos, the objective is to extend rainfall through the dry season (which began in November and continues through April or May), keeping the ground as near the saturation point as possible and obstructing traffic that normally fords streams during the low water period.

A corollary phase of the operation would be to conduct intensified weather reconnaissance and additional experiments in weather modification over international waters in the South China Sea, from Philippine bases—one principal objective being the development of techniques to dissipate cloud cover as well as to induce abnormal rainfall.

The impact on civilian population will be much the same, in kind, and greater in degree, than that discussed below with respect to areas outside the target zones. The psychological impact will be perhaps greater than any other effect, particularly when conditions characteristic of the rainy season are unexpected.

We came up with a few dandy ideas that include murdering innocent people, blaming it on Cuba, and starting a real humdinger of a war! Which do you prefer, Mr. President?

Operation
NORTHWOODS

During a tense period in American foreign policy, an influential group proposed a radical plan to manipulate public sentiment to justify military action in Cuba.

TOP SECRET — SPECIAL HANDLING — NOFORN

THE JOINT CHIEFS OF STAFF
WASHINGTON 25, D.C.

UNCLASSIFIED   13 March 1962

MEMORANDUM FOR THE SECRETARY OF DEFENSE

Subject: Justification for US Military Intervention in Cuba (TS)

1. The Joint Chiefs of Staff have considered the attached Memorandum for the Chief of Operations, Cuba Project, which responds to a request of that office for brief but precise description of pretexts which would provide justification for US military intervention in Cuba.

2. The Joint Chiefs of Staff recommend that the proposed memorandum be forwarded as a preliminary submission suitable for planning purposes. It is assumed that there will be similar submissions from other agencies and that these inputs will be used as a basis for developing a time-phased plan. Individual projects can then be considered on a case-by-case basis.

3. Further, it is assumed that a single agency will be given the primary responsibility for developing military and para-military aspects of the basic plan. It is recommended that this responsibility be assigned the Joint Chiefs of Staff.

For the Joint Chiefs of Staff:

SYSTEMATICALLY REVIEWED
BY JCS ON
CLASSIFICATION CONTINUED

L. L. LEMNITZER
Chairman
Joint Chiefs of Staff

1 Enclosure
Memo for Chief of Operations, Cuba Project

EXCLUDED FROM GDS

EXCLUDED FROM AUTOMATIC
REGRADING: DOD DIR 5200.10
DOES NOT APPLY

On June 4, 1962, a makeshift raft carrying twenty-five men, women, and children fleeing Communist Cuba and the reign of terror of its dictator-president Fidel Castro had just been spotted from the southernmost tip of Florida when the unthinkable happened. The boat suddenly burst into flames with debris shooting in all directions and terrified refugees knocked unconscious and thrown into the shark-infested waters. A US Coast Guard rescue crew was scrambled, but by the time they were able to reach the smoking debris, there were no survivors.

Just three days later, an explosion rocked downtown Miami. A moving van, converted into a mobile time bomb, had been detonated in the middle of rush-hour traffic. Thirteen people were killed, and dozens more injured. Preliminary intelligence reports pointed to the attack being the work of Cuban operatives who had been sent to kill American civilians—a bold show of force meant to intimidate President Kennedy as he sought to keep the Communists from spreading their deadly ideology across the globe.

The American people were deeply saddened to hear of the deaths of the refugees on the raft. They held candlelight vigils and arranged a memorial service to commemorate the senseless act of violence that took the lives of innocent people simply trying to find a better life. But when the fight was brought to American soil—when the small, Russia-backed country just ninety miles from Florida killed innocent Americans as they traveled home from work—it went beyond sad speeches and candlelight memorials. Now, there was anger.

Within days a full-scale military invasion of Cuba was authorized. The mission: to topple the Communist regime, try Castro and his generals as war criminals, and install a democratic government that would stabilize the region and return peace and prosperity to the Cuban people. Americans cheered as they gathered around their black and white TVs and watched the battlegroup set sail.

Things Aren't Always What They Seem

Thankfully, these tragedies never actually happened. But it's frightening how close they came to being a reality.

In the early 1960s, at the height of the Cold War, the US government developed a plan to launch a series of false flag attacks on American soil and civilian targets. These attacks would be used as a pretext for launching a full-scale war against Cuba, which was viewed by some as a growing threat to American interests. The plan, known as Operation Northwoods, was ultimately rejected by President Kennedy, but it offers an important glimpse into the lengths that some officials were willing to go in order to manufacture public support for military action against foreign enemies.

A false flag attack is an operation undertaken by one country or group in order to appear as though it has been carried out by another country or group. False flag attacks are often used to drum up support for military action against an enemy. In the case of Northwoods, the US government was considering carrying out false flag attacks on American soil in order to win public support for a war against Cuba.

Those proposing this plan weren't low-level bureaucrats or random politicians. The proposal came in 1962 from the

Joint Chiefs of Staff—the top military leaders in the country who had sworn an oath to uphold the Constitution and defend Americans. Now they proposed *killing* some of them to falsely blame their murder on others in hopes of shifting public opinion by deceiving the public.

Together with officers from the "intelligence" community, these top-ranking officers drafted a document called "Justification for US Military Intervention in Cuba." The document outlined a series of proposals for how the United States could create conditions that would justify taking military action against Cuba. These proposals included carrying out terrorist attacks in Miami and other US cities and sinking boats of Cuban refugees fleeing the country, as part of a "Communist Cuban terror campaign."

When President Kennedy found out about Northwoods, he was reportedly horrified. He immediately halted the plans and issued an order that no further actions were to be taken without his express approval. In the years since Kennedy's assassination, some people have claimed that he was killed because he refused to go along with Northwoods. While there is little evidence to support this theory, we do know that military leaders were unhappy with the president's refusal to implement their plan.

Cui Bono?

Many in the government, including most high-ranking military officials, feared that the Russians were trying to use Communist Cuba to attack or otherwise harm the United States. It seemed that all diplomatic avenues were failing, and the prospect of an ever-strengthening Communist power just ninety miles off the coast of Florida was a source of much anxiety for US officials.

It is obviously considered undiplomatic to invade another country, or topple its government, simply because you don't like the way they do things and you feel like they're too close. But that is essentially what many in power wanted to do. They just had to find a tricky way to do it that would make it *look* as though they were defending themselves—like *they* were the victims of aggression instead of the aggressors. Scheming minds set to work to think up every possible way the United States could justify attacking Cuba and replacing its government with one they liked better. Thankfully, these individuals did *not* benefit from their proposed conspiracy because President Kennedy rejected their plans—but what if he hadn't?

What if the president had agreed with all of his advisers and given the go-ahead for US officials to attack a raft of Cuban refugees in the midst of their perilous journey across shark-infested waters in search of peace and prosperity for themselves and their families, and what if they'd succeeded in making it look like Fidel Castro had ordered the attack? Would the American people have been angry enough to support war? Would we know the truth today about who really killed them, or would we have all been taught for decades that it was the work of the nefarious Communists in Cuba?

And what would have happened if we had gone to war with Cuba? Would Russia have supported them and entered into open warfare with the United States? Would one or both countries have used nuclear weapons? How different would the world look today if Russia and the United States had fought a war over Cuba?

There are many examples of false flag operations employed as justification for war. Those who plan and carry them out always imagine that they can manipulate and control others into giving them the results they are hoping for, but this rarely—if ever—happens. Usually the result is loss of life and a deeper distrust of the government by the people.

Why Does This Matter?

Northwoods continues to be studied and debated by historians as a troubling reminder of what can happen when paranoia and fear take hold among those in power. There will always be people or organizations that are viewed as threats both at home and abroad, but it's important to remember the lessons of Northwoods and remain vigilant against those who would seek to use our fears to further their own agendas.

For example, in the winter of 2003, experts feverishly testified before Congress, and the media ran nonstop messaging about the dangers posed by Saddam Hussein and the "weapons of mass destruction" that he was said to be amassing. It was necessary, they insisted, that the US invade Iraq to oust Hussein and destroy his dangerous chemical and biological weaponry.

The war lasted thirteen years, the government of Iraq was toppled, hundreds of thousands of people were killed, and the supposed weapons of mass destruction that Americans were told would be found were not.

Similar to the stories of the Gulf of Tonkin incident, or Nayirah's testimony, or Operation Northwoods, there is a pattern of behavior amongst US intelligence agencies, high-ranking military officers, and other government officials in which fabrications, false flags, and outright lies are used to justify going to war. It is unlikely that their efforts stopped after the Iraq War, but it is possible that they have altered their methods a little.

What do we believe to be true today that actually isn't?

What "official report" was fabricated, based on total lies that were premeditated by government officials, intended to deceive the public into believing something different and thus acting differently?

How can we even know what is true, when our own government is so willing to feed us lies?

Finally, can we honestly conclude that the government isn't doing things like this today?

What We Learned

1. The use of "false flag" operations has been discussed and planned in detail since at least the early 1960s.

2. Governments will lie, fake attacks against their country, and even kill innocent people in order to create public support when they want to go to war.

3. The very military officers who are supposed to protect the American people are sometimes willing to kill some of them if it's for the "greater good."

Justification for Military Intervention in Cuba

Memorandum for the Secretary of Defense

March 13, 1962

It is recognized that any action which becomes pretext for US military intervention in Cuba will lead to a political decision which then would lead to military action.

The suggested courses of action... are based on the premise that US military intervention will result from a period of heightened US-Cuban tensions which place the United States in the position of suffering justifiable grievances. World opinion, and the United Nations forum should be favorably affected by developing the international image of the Cuban government as rash and irresponsible, and as an alarming and unpredictable threat to the peace of the Western Hemisphere.

Since it would seem desirable to use legitimate provocation as the basis for US military intervention in Cuba a cover and deception plan... could be executed as an initial effort to provoke Cuban reactions. Harassment plus deceptive actions to convince the Cubans of imminent invasion would be emphasized. Our military posture throughout execution of the plan will allow a rapid change from exercise to intervention if Cuban response justifies.

A series of well coordinated incidents will be planned to take place in and around Guantanamo to give genuine appearance of being done by hostile Cuban forces.

Incidents to establish a credible attack (not in chronological order):

1. Start rumors (many). Use clandestine radio.
2. Land friendly Cubans in uniform "over-the-fence" to stage attack on base.
3. Capture Cuban (friendly) saboteurs inside the base.
4. Start riots near the base main gate (friendly Cubans).
5. Blow up ammunition inside the base; start fires.
6. Burn aircraft on air base (sabotage).
7. Lob mortar shells from outside of base into base. Some damage to installations.
8. capture assault teams approaching from the sea or vicinity of Guantanamo City.
9. Capture militia group which storms the base.
10. Sabotage ship in harbor; large fires — napthalene.
11. Sink ship near harbor entrance. Conduct funerals for mock-victims

A "Remember the Maine" incident could be arranged in several forms. We could blow up a US ship in Guantanamo Bay and blame Cuba. We could blow up a drone (unmanned) vessel anywhere in the Cuban waters.

We could develop a Communist Cuban terror campaign in the Miami area, in other Florida cities and even in Washington. The terror campaign could be pointed at refugees seeking haven in the United States. We could sink a boatload of Cubans enroute to Florida (real or simulated). We could foster attempts on lives of Cuban refugees in the United States even to the extent of wounding in instances to be widely publicized. Exploding a few plastic bombs in carefully chosen spots, the arrest of Cuban agents and the release of prepared documents substantiating Cuban involvement, also would be helpful in projecting the idea of an irresponsible government.

These study results will ruin our sugar profits!
Conclusive Dietary Study
Diet In Relation to Obesity and Heart Disease
Fat
Sugar Intake
Illness
Fat
Finding: high sugar diet causes
obesity &
Have our own scientists make these edits and then send a new paper to the scientific journals.

SUGAR/FAT
Studies

A powerful industry used its financial resources to direct research and alter Americans' understanding of what makes us sick.

% of Obese American Adults

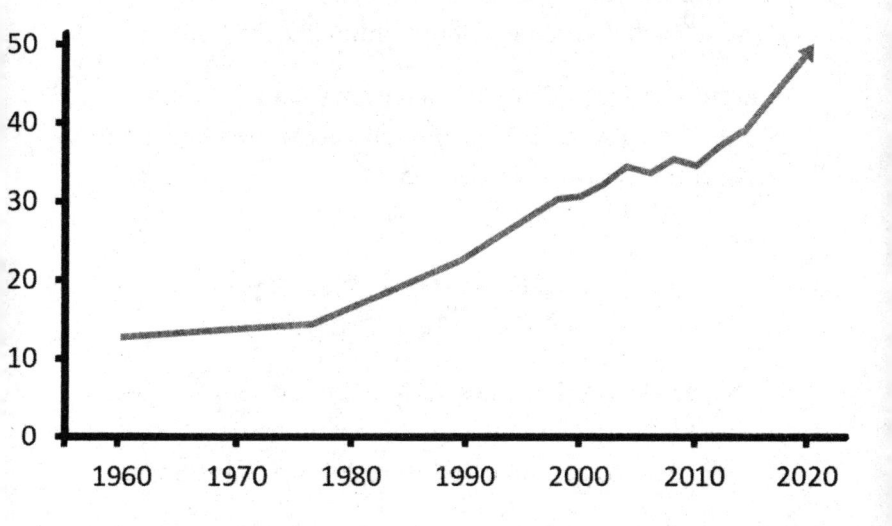

In the early 1960s, multiple studies showed that sugar was likely a contributing factor in the growing health problems facing Americans. Certain that their product was harmless and wanting to assure people that they could safely continue indulging in their favorite treats, the Sugar Research Foundation (SRF) decided to respond. Its aim was to thoroughly investigate any possibility that sugar was causing Americans to become fat and sick—a claim that they were certain was based on flawed studies, so a second purpose of the Foundation was to double-check the accuracy of the studies that had concluded sugar was unhealthy.

Rigorous research was conducted by unbiased parties, and not only were the anti-sugar studies found to have been flawed, but the *actual* culprit was discovered. Americans, it turned out, were getting fat and sick because they ate too much fat. Medical journals published the findings, and doctors began reforming the health advice they gave their patients. Sugar was fine, they counseled, but the animal fats, butters, and whole milks and creams that had been a staple of American diets since the country's founding had been confirmed dangerous by professionals. Efforts were made to curb their consumption immediately.

Americans eagerly complied, a new market was opened, and the "low fat/fat free" revolution had begun. Americans were on their way to healthier living.

Things Aren't Always What They Seem

Big Sugar's Deception dates back to the early 1960s when studies first began linking sugar to heart disease. In response, the Sugar Association (then known as the Sugar

Research Foundation) launched a public relations campaign aimed at discrediting these studies and protecting sugar's reputation.

First, they went on the offensive against any science that dared suggest sugar was anything other than a healthy part of the human diet. They did this by paying researchers to write articles critiquing any study critical of sugar. These pro-sugar articles were then published in scientific journals, giving them an aura of legitimacy.

They also needed a scapegoat. One of the most egregious things the SRF did was to fund a research review that argued that the primary culprit in coronary heart disease was rising cholesterol levels from saturated fats. The researchers claimed that the science connecting sugar to coronary heart disease was "limited" and that a patient's sugar consumption shouldn't be considered in an assessment for developing heart disease. This study was published in 1967 in the *New England Journal of Medicine*, and it shaped public policy—and public perceptions—about diet and heart disease for decades to come. It triggered a low-fat diet craze that continued for decades, resulting in Americans consuming even more processed foods and sugars as they attempted to avoid fat. As a result, Americans now eat and drink more sugar than ever before, and chronic disease rates are higher than ever.

Finally, when all else failed, the sugar industry used its considerable political clout to dismantle any government regulations or policies that might have restricted their profits. For example, they lobbied hard against mandatory nutrition labels that would list the amount of sugar in a product. As a result of their efforts, it wasn't until 1990 that nutrition labels became mandatory in the United States—and even then, they still didn't have to list the amount of added sugars.

For decades, the sugar industry has worked tirelessly to control the narrative around its product. By discrediting scientific studies, conducting their own "independent" research, and using their political clout to influence regulation, they've managed to keep Americans hooked on sugary foods and beverages—regardless of how harmful those products might be for their health—while purposely steering people away from foods that keep them healthy and fit.

Cui Bono?

Imagine if you made a product that you knew would make people fat and sick, you didn't really care if your product made people fat and sick, and you had a lot of money. Now imagine that you heard that there was research being conducted that was going to reveal to the world that your product made people fat and sick. How would you act?

Of course this is difficult for a thoughtful and caring person to imagine, but this was the exact situation that Big Sugar found themselves in. They couldn't risk people learning the truth about their product, so they used their money and influence to change the outcome of the studies they could and conduct their own studies—of dubious scientific credibility—to refute the ones they couldn't change.

In the end, their sugar-coated scheme worked. People were tricked into believing fat was bad for them and that sugar was not to blame for American obesity, heart disease, and overall poor health. But what if Big Sugar was right? What if it really was those pesky fats and not the refined and empty carbs that sugar provided? How would we know?

Up until the '60s, American diets consisted of healthy fats, carbs, and fruits and vegetables; sugar was seen as a treat but certainly not something to be consumed in large quantities or even every day. Since Americans adopted a diet low in fat and high in grains and sugars, what do you think has happened to their overall health? Has it improved like it should have if sugar was okay to eat and fats were bad for you? It has not. In fact, Americans have grown fatter, sicker, and more chronically ill.

Big Sugar may have won the battle, but a lot of people are waking up to their lies and taking charge of their own health and happiness by returning to the way people ate before dishonest mega-industries manipulated "the science" for their own gain and at the expense of the people who trust them.

Why Does This Matter?

Conspiracies aren't exclusive to government. While this book focuses mostly on the conspiring actions of those with political power, plenty of people with financial or business power can and do secretly conspire with others (often the media and government) to further their goals.

It was relatively easy, in 1960, for a multimillion-dollar industry to manipulate scientific research and pressure researchers into publishing findings that told a not-quite-true version of the studies. There was also a lot of crossover between those who had a financial interest in seeing Big Sugar come out looking "sweet" and those who were supposed to be conducting impartial research. For example, one of the researchers, the chairman of Harvard's Public Health Nutrition Department, was also on the board of the Sugar Research Foundation. This crossover effect has only increased in the years since the sugar studies, and now it is commonplace to find those with something to gain, or something to hide, being in positions of influence over the very organizations that are supposed to be overseeing them.

For example, the CDC is supposed to oversee public health and recommend what types of vaccines should be given to children and young adults. They are supposed to be an impartial body that makes recommendations based on their interpretation of scientific research. But the CDC owns the patents on vaccine technology for several vaccines, which earns them millions of dollars every year. That doesn't sound very impartial. Likewise, there is practically a revolving door between high-level employees at companies that manufacture and develop vaccines and government agencies that recommend vaccines or manage public health. This means that when someone runs a pharmaceutical company for a long time, they will commonly retire from that job and take a new position with a government agency that decides which pharmaceutical products to recommend to the public.

The conspirators in the sugar study also discovered something that would change the way corporations and special interest groups manipulate the public and market their products while looking uninvolved and impartial. They found that if they targeted medical journals—peer reviewed publications that were non-political, science-based, and data-driven—then people would unquestioningly accept whatever they read—or whatever the news reported or their doctors told them, since most people don't actually read scientific journals. Big Sugar didn't have to refute the bad news about their product or hire PR teams to pay for new messaging in their marketing efforts—they simply manipulated the science.

And after all, who would question science?

A conspiracy involving increased sugar consumption may appear trivial at first, but it's worth noting that heavy sugar consumption leads to nearly 200,000 deaths annually due to diabetes, cardiovascular disease, and cancer. To put this into perspective, this figure is over 15 times the number of Americans who lost their lives during World War II. Suddenly, the issue seems far more significant, doesn't it?

What We Learned

1. Medical and scientific research can be manipulated by powerful groups who don't want the truth about their products to be known or who want a specific outcome.

2. Conspiracies aren't exclusive to the government; powerful and wealthy people can still conspire secretly to advance their agendas.

3. The science is never "settled" because we are always learning new things, and sometimes the science we thought was settled turns out to be fake—bought and paid for by groups who have something to gain or something to lose!

Sugar Industry and Coronary Heart Disease Research

A Historical Analysis of Internal Industry Documents
Published in the *Journal of the American Medical Assoc.*

November 2016

Sugar Research Foundation (SRF) president Henry Hass's 1954 speech, "What's New in Sugar Research," to the American Society of Sugar Beet Technologists identified a strategic opportunity for the sugar industry: increase sugar's market share by getting Americans to eat a lower-fat diet: "Leading nutritionists are pointing out the chemical connection between [American's] high-fat diet and the formation of cholesterol which partly plugs our arteries and capillaries, restricts the flow of blood, and causes high blood pressure and heart trouble... if you put [the middle-aged man] on a low-fat diet, it takes just five days for the blood cholesterol to get down to where it should be... If the carbohydrate industries were to recapture this 20 percent of the calories in the US diet (the difference between the 40 percent which fat has and the 20 percent which it ought to have) and if sugar maintained its present share of the carbohydrate market, this change would mean an increase in the per capita consumption of sugar more than a third with a tremendous improvement in general health."

The industry would subsequently spend $600,000 ($5.3 million in 2016 dollars) to teach "people who had never had a course in biochemistry... that sugar is what keeps every human being alive and with energy to face our daily problems."

[SRF vice president John] Hickson recommended that SRF fund CHD [coronary heart disease] research: "We should carefully review the reports, probably with a committee of nutrition specialists; see what weak points there are in the experimentation, and replicate the studies with appropriate corrections. Then we can publish the data and refute our detractors."

These internal documents show that the SRF initiated CHD research in 1965 to protect market share and that its first project, a literature review, was published in NEJM [the *New England Journal of Medicine*] in 1967 without disclosure of the sugar industry's funding or role. The NEJM review served the sugar industry's interests by arguing that epidemiologic, animal, and mechanistic studies associating sucrose with CHD were limited, implying they should not be included in an evidentiary assessment of the CHD risks of sucrose.

Following the NEJM review, the sugar industry continued to fund research on CHD and other chronic diseases "as a main prop of the industry's defense." For example, in 1971, it influenced the National Institute of Dental Research's National Caries Program to shift its emphasis to dental caries interventions other than restricting sucrose. The industry commissioned a review, "Sugar in the Diet of Man," which it credited with, among other industry tactics, favorably influencing the 1976 US Food and Drug Administration evaluation of the safety of sugar. These findings, our analysis, and current Sugar Association criticisms of evidence linking sucrose to cardiovascular disease suggest the industry may have a long history of influencing federal policy.

You will have no privacy, own nothing, and be happy!
All must obey.

The GREAT RESET

Never letting a crisis go to waste, influential individuals proposed completely restructuring the global economy in the wake of COVID-19.

WORLD ECONOMIC FORUM

The Great Reset is a term used to describe the need for a fundamental change to the way our world works. Many individuals, particularly those in positions of power, have serious concerns about the structure of our economy, the state of the climate, and the income inequality that plagues mankind.

For some time, these elitists have been pushing for radical changes that would reorder the economy and create more "equity"—all in the name of helping the least among us. And, recalling the words of their colleague Rahm Emanuel—former president Barack Obama's advisor—they wanted to "never let a good crisis go to waste." When COVID-19 erupted onto the world scene, many of these leaders, particularly those affiliated with the World Economic Forum (WEF), saw an opportunity to promote their vision of a different future and enact policies that would help bring it about—again, all in the name of shaping the future for the better.

The Great Reset is sometimes referred to as "The Fourth Industrial Revolution" or "The Great Transformation." It refers to the idea that we are on the cusp of a new era where technology will drastically change the way we live and work. For example, we are already seeing self-driving cars and AI-powered chatbots become more common. Imagine a world where all of our products are made using sustainable materials and everyone has access to clean energy. Think of a future where you don't have to spend so much of your time working for the money you earn, or the home you live in, and a future where people who don't have the same skills as other people are given a fair shot. That's the kind of world the Great Reset envisions. It's all about opportunity and equity.

The Great Reset is an initiative launched by the WEF with supporters like King Charles III, Bill Gates, Angela Merkel, and other politicians and celebrities who portray themselves as saviors of mankind, concerned for others' welfare—and not at all concerned about power and wealth. Its goal is to reset the world after the COVID-19 pandemic by addressing some of the world's most pressing issues.

In particular, the Great Reset focuses on creating a more equitable and sustainable future for all. This includes addressing issues like climate change, racism, and inequality. To achieve these goals, the Great Reset proposes policies like the Green New Deal, Universal Basic Income, and free health care for all.

The Great Reset crusaders point to big problems they're trying to solve. They highlight climate change and its alleged ravaging of the Earth's ecosystems, with extreme weather events more common and costing trillions of dollars in damages. They also point out systemic racism that disadvantages people of color and drives inequality. Finally, they point to significant income inequality that has reached levels not seen since before the Great Depression.

Things Aren't Always What They Seem

It is true that the Great Reset is sometimes referred to as "The Fourth Industrial Revolution" or "The Great Transformation." But far from being something to celebrate, or welcome, this proposed new era is one where technology and government will drastically change the way we live and work, and where all of the "old" things—to include the way we think and act, and our basic freedoms—will be replaced with newer (and often worse) things.

Sure, there have been industrial revolutions in the past, and they have (for the most part) improved the quality of life for most people. The difference between this revolution and others is that the Great Reset is being imposed on the world from a top-down power structure. In previous industrial revolutions, the world changed organically—with people and industries adapting to new inventions and new ways of doing things, whereby the world was set on a new course through voluntary action and innovation.

This time, the world's wealthiest business owners, politicians, and celebrities—the elite who have power and want more of it—have conspired to lay a path *for* the world, whether the world asked for it (or wanted it) or not.

Among the chief proponents of the Great Reset is Klaus Schwab, founder and executive director of the WEF, who published in a 1973 manifesto his idea that companies should value "stakeholders" instead of shareholders. So-called "stakeholder capitalism" is an economic system in which businesses are accountable to all of their stakeholders—not just shareholders. This includes employees, customers, suppliers, and the communities in which they operate.

On the surface, this might sound like a good thing. After all, businesses should be accountable to everyone they interact with, right? Not quite. Stakeholder capitalism is bad for both businesses and society as a whole.

When businesses are required to answer to multiple stakeholders, it makes them less efficient and less profitable. This is because businesses are forced to focus on short-term goals that please multiple stakeholders instead of long-term goals that create value for shareholders. Answering to multiple bosses makes things confusing and prevents you from focusing on what will work best.

For example, imagine that a company is considering two different investment opportunities. One investment would create long-term value for shareholders but would require laying off some employees in the short-term. The other investment would avoid layoffs but would not create as much shareholder value. Under stakeholder capitalism, the company would likely choose the second investment because layoffs would hurt employees (a key stakeholder group). However, this decision would actually be bad for the business because it would lead to lower profits and possibly affect sustainability in the long run.

Stakeholder capitalism also hurts individuals by making them less free and less prosperous by giving too much power to government bureaucrats and special interest groups at the expense of individual rights. For example, suppose that you're a small business owner who wants to expand your business by opening up a new storefront. Under stakeholder capitalism, government officials might deny you a permit and shut down your project, citing their concern that expansion would "clutter up the neighborhood." They think they know what's best for you and your business—that they're looking out for the "greater good" and considering the wishes of the "stakeholders" in the community. In contrast, under free market capitalism, you would be able to open up your new storefront without any interference from government bureaucrats. It's a question of who gets to decide.

But Schwab's ideas go beyond this idea of stakeholder capitalism. There is a push for an economic restructuring by the WEF as part of its annual Davos conference hosting the world's elitists. In June 2020, as the COVID-19 pandemic was still growing, they published an article saying there is "an urgent need for global stakeholders to cooperate in simultaneously managing the direct consequences of the COVID-19 crisis." This article was the launch of their "Great Reset initiative" where they and their political puppets would "build a new social contract that honors the dignity of every human being." And in a book titled *COVID-19: The Great Reset*, Schwab said that the government's response should "revamp all aspects of our societies and economies, from education to social contracts and working conditions." In other words, they would exert more government control to restrict people's freedoms to shape society in their preferred fashion.

The WEF is just one organization of many, and certainly they and their leader are free to propose whatever crazy idea they wish. But the Great Reset concept wasn't just shouted into the air—it became the marching orders for many worldwide leaders who take their cue from these institutions, much like a hive of bees acting each independently, but collectively in concert with the queen.

In 2017, Schwab openly boasted about the WEF's ability to "penetrate the cabinets" of governments around the world, installing loyal individuals in positions of power who would act upon the recommendations of the organization—people like Canadian Prime Minister Justin Trudeau, former New Zealand prime minister Jacinda Ardern, French President Emmanuel Macron, and former UK prime minister Tony Blair, among many others.

This organization, whose mission proudly boasts engaging "the foremost political, business, cultural and other leaders of society to shape global, regional and industry agendas," has also called for "a new world order."

Cui Bono?

Socialists like to claim that their economic ideas would create more equality and fairness, yet every time a socialist system has existed, poor people become poorer, and most of the country's wealth is taken by those in power and their friends. Klaus Schwab's proposal to "revamp all aspects of our societies and economies" is similar. While he and the WEF may claim that it is to "honor the dignity of every human being," the reality will always be the opposite. Only freedom provides true dignity and opportunity for everyone involved.

Ida Auken is a "Young Global Leader" for the WEF—someone who will likely be groomed to "penetrate the cabinets" of various governments. In an article envisioning her ideal future, published by WEF in 2016, Auken wrote, "Welcome to 2030: I own nothing, have no privacy, and life has never been better." She describes the purported benefits of having no car or appliances or clothes. "Once in a while I get annoyed about the fact that I have no real privacy. Nowhere I can go and not be registered. I know that, somewhere, everything I do, think and dream of is recorded. I just hope that nobody will use it against me."

Despite this dystopian dream, Auken wrote, "All in all, it is a good life," but one in which private property no longer exists, nor does privacy—an Orwellian nightmare. And this answers the question, *cui bono?* Those benefiting, like in all socialist-style systems, are those in power. These elites will most certainly own a home and clothing and a car. They will have a large degree of privacy. They'll be protected by armed personnel and able to control their own destiny far more than the rest of society that is at the state's mercy. It's good to be at the top of the pyramid of power.

There are several ways in which the elites in society stand to benefit from the Great Reset. First, it would give them more control over the global economy. By centralizing political and economic power in the hands of a small elite, decisions affecting the lives of billions would be made without direct accountability to the public. It'd be a central planning nightmare. This effort would also require a massive redistribution of wealth, making the problems of income inequality even worse. And restructuring the economy in this way would require significant surveillance of people's economic activities—such as with a central bank digital currency or social credit system, where individuals can be restricted from buying things or traveling places if they are found to be insufficiently supportive of the government's goals.

Why Does This Matter?

There are people like Klaus Schwab who work quietly, patiently, and largely behind the scenes for years. And then a moment arrives that provides them an opportunity to advance their agenda by leaps and bounds. That was the case with COVID-19; though WEF had been around for half a century, its shining moment was when there were so many global challenges all at once. Schwab and other elitists capitalized on that opportunity to push their proposals and obtain more political power.

But the Great Reset really matters because if any of its proposals are enacted by its "penetrated" politicians and bureaucrats who coordinate their efforts across the globe, it will drastically change your life (unless you're privileged to be part of the elite). Here are some ways it could affect you:

- Rising costs as a result of restrictions or outright bans on fossil fuels, which Great Reset proponents believe change the climate.

- Rising inflation to pay for big government programs designed to restructure the economy, transferring wealth from individual savers to the bankers and politicians, who benefit from the newly created money before inflation's effects are fully realized.

- Decreasing privacy as governments monitor the economic activity and lives of its citizens in order to nudge them toward preferred behavior, as is seen in China's social credit system.

- Loss of freedom as local government is weakened through the consolidation of power in national and global governments so central planners can more easily affect the lives of the masses.

- Reduced innovation and productivity as entrepreneurs are restricted from building wealth as a result of "stakeholder capitalism" initiatives that limit their options and regulate their business choices.

What We Learned

1. Emergencies and crises like COVID-19 are an opportunity for conspiring people to advance their agenda more aggressively than they could before, since people are scared and want someone with a plan to fix the problem.

2. Government policies are often presented under the guise of "for the greater good," but at their core they are often intended to limit your freedom and grow the government's power and reach.

3. Not everyone believes that freedom, liberty, and the ability to live and work without coercion is good. There are many powerful people who see those things as dangers to their power and want to severely limit human independence and freedom.

4. The WEF has "penetrated the cabinets" of governments around the world, installing loyal individuals in positions of power who conspire together to advance agendas like the Great Reset.

The Great Reset

A World Economic Forum announcement

June 2020

"The Great Reset" will be the theme of a unique twin summit to be convened by the World Economic Forum in January 2021. The 51st World Economic Forum Annual Meeting will bring together global leaders from government, business and civil society, and stakeholders from around the world in a unique configuration that includes both in-person and virtual dialogues.

"We only have one planet and we know that climate change could be the next global disaster with even more dramatic consequences for humankind. We have to decarbonize the economy in the short window still remaining and bring our thinking and behaviour once more into harmony with nature," said Klaus Schwab, Founder and Executive Chairman of the World Economic Forum.

"In order to secure our future and to prosper, we need to evolve our economic model and put people and planet at the heart of global value creation. If there is one critical lesson to learn from this crisis, it is that we need to put nature at the heart of how we operate. We simply can't waste more time," said HRH The Prince of Wales.

"The Great Reset is a welcome recognition that this human tragedy must be a wake-up call. We must build more equal, inclusive and sustainable economies and societies that are more resilient in the face of pandemics, climate change and the many other global changes we face," said António Guterres, Secretary-General, United Nations, New York.

"A Great Reset is necessary to build a new social contract that honours the dignity of every human being," added Schwab. "The global health crisis has laid bare the unsustainability of our old system in terms of social cohesion, the lack of equal opportunities and inclusiveness. Nor can we turn our backs on the evils of racism and discrimination. We need to build into this new social contract our intergenerational responsibility to ensure that we live up to the expectations of young people."

"COVID-19 has accelerated our transition into the age of the Fourth Industrial Revolution. We have to make sure that the new technologies in the digital, biological and physical world remain human-centred and serve society as a whole, providing everyone with fair access," he said.

"This global pandemic has also demonstrated again how interconnected we are. We have to restore a functioning system of smart global cooperation structured to address the challenges of the next 50 years. The Great Reset will require us to integrate all stakeholders of global society into a community of common interest, purpose and action," said Schwab. "We need a change of mindset, moving from short-term to long-term thinking, moving from shareholder capitalism to stakeholder responsibility. Environmental, social and good governance have to be a measured part of corporate and governmental accountability," he added.

This innovative summit will... provide a unique opportunity at the beginning of 2021 to bring together the key global government and business leaders in Davos, yet framed within a global multistakeholder summit driven by the younger generation to ensure that the Great Reset dialogue pushes beyond the boundaries of traditional thinking and is truly forward-oriented.

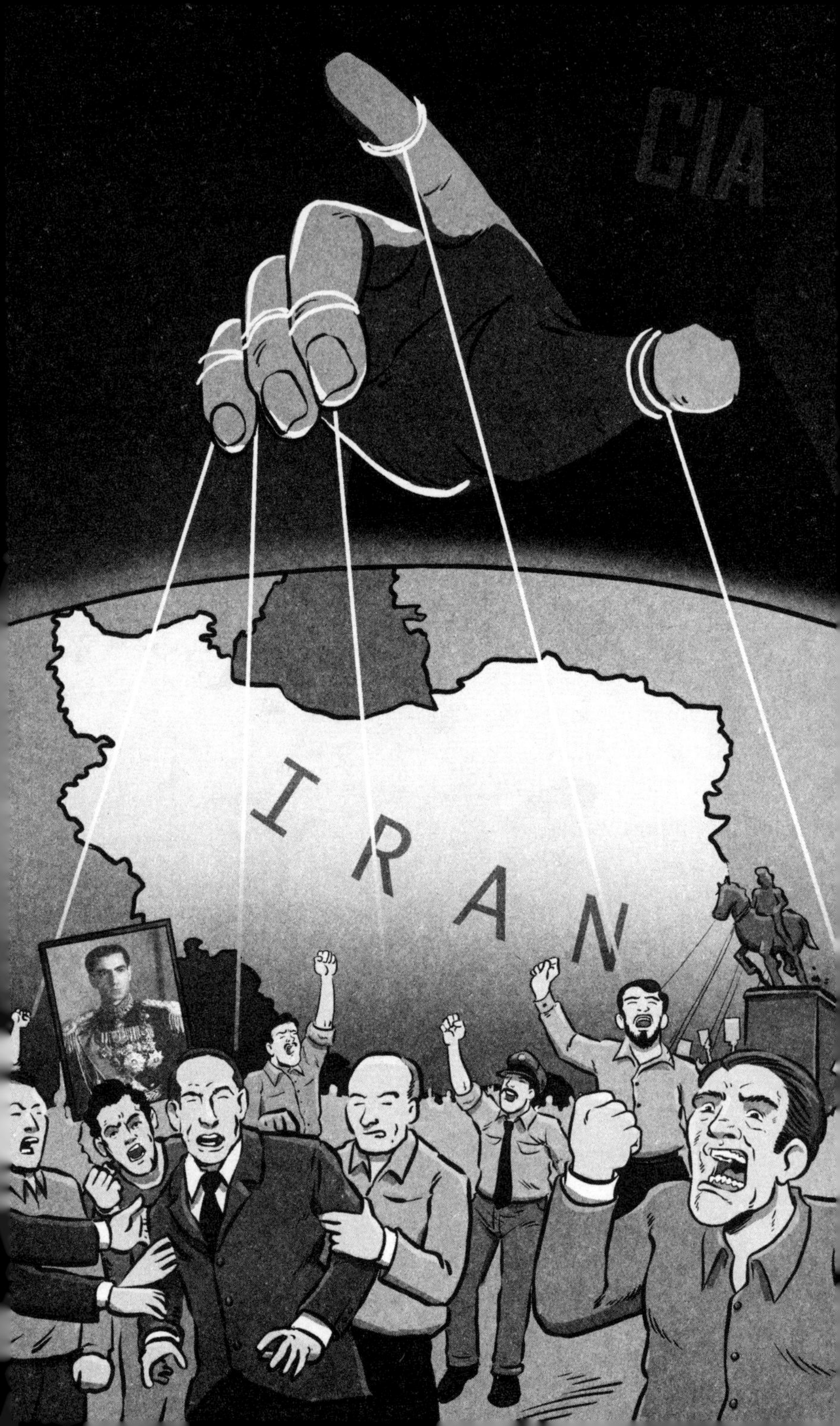
CIA
IRAN

Operation AJAX

Dark forces conspired to alter Iran's destiny, setting a course for chaos, resentment, and a revolution that shook the world.

ON THIS DAY IN 1953

BROOKLYN EAGLE

MOSSADEGH IS OUSTED
Overthrown by Army in Bloody Coup
Ike Holds Parleys Here — MOB BURNS HIS HOME, BUTCHERS LOYAL AIDE

GIVES BOOST TO RIEGELMAN AND CITY GOP

Stephen J. Carney, 45, Dies Ex-Water Chief, Dem Boss

COPS, FBI HOT ON TRAIL OF BANK ROBBER

For 444 days, from November 4, 1979, to January 20, 1981, fifty-two Americans were held hostage by Iranian militants. Fourteen additional Americans had been taken hostage initially but were later released. The hostages were subjected to humiliating treatment and brutally interrogated while their families back home lived in fear, not knowing if their loved ones were alive or dead.

It all began when a group of Iranian students stormed the US Embassy in Tehran and took the American diplomats and citizens inside as hostages. The students were angry over the decision by President Jimmy Carter to allow the deposed Shah of Iran, Mohammad Reza Pahlavi, into the United States for cancer treatment.

The students demanded that the Shah be returned to Iran to face justice, but Carter refused. In response, the Iranian students announced that they would hold the hostages until the Shah was returned to Iran. As news of the crisis spread, other Iranians began joining the students at the embassy compound.

The conditions inside quickly deteriorated as the militants became more aggressive and abusive toward their captives. The hostages were kept in small rooms and blindfolded or made to wear hoods over their heads whenever they were moved. They were denied access to medical care, and some were beaten or put through mock executions.

Meanwhile, back in Washington, D.C., President Carter was under immense pressure to resolve the situation before it spun further out of control. He initially tried to negotiate a peaceful resolution, but when that failed he authorized a risky military rescue operation called Operation Eagle Claw.

Eagle Claw was an attempt to rescue the hostages using military force, but it ended in disaster when a helicopter crashed into a transport plane, killing eight American servicemen. The failure of this mission only served to make matters worse and finally led Carter to begin seriously negotiating with the Iranian government for a peaceful resolution.

After months of difficult negotiations, an agreement was finally reached and on January 20, 1981, exactly 444 days after they were taken captive, the remaining fifty-two American hostages were released. In exchange for their freedom, Carter agreed to unfreeze Iranian assets worth over $7 billion that had been seized by the US government as part of economic sanctions against Iran.

Things Aren't Always What They Seem

Mohammad Mossadegh became prime minister of Iran in 1951 just as his government was nationalizing the Iranian oil industry, which until that point had been controlled by the British-owned Anglo-Iranian Oil Company (AIOC). Mossadegh was an Iranian politician and lawyer, and the people of Iran liked him. The nationalization of the oil industry was popular with the Iranian people but angered the British government, which saw it as an act of economic warfare. In response, the AIOC organized a worldwide embargo of Iranian oil.

The Eisenhower administration initially refused to get involved but changed its mind after receiving intelligence that Mossadegh was planning to align Iran with the Soviet

Union. Prompted by the British, the CIA hatched a plan to overthrow Mossadegh, who was elected by Iran's Parliament, and install the Shah, or king, as absolute ruler of Iran. The project was named Operation Ajax and included activities such as bribing Iranian politicians, planting false stories in the media, and even orchestrating mob violence.

In early 1953, the CIA orchestrated a coup, partnering with supporters of Fazlollah Zahedi and the Shah to overthrow Mossadegh. The CIA saw Mossadegh as a threat to their interests in the Middle East, which included access to and control of the oil supply. Their plan to lead a coup was "conceived and approved at the highest levels of government."

Mossadegh also opposed Western military presence in Iran and sought to limit their influence. He established closer ties with the Soviet Union, which the United States felt posed a threat to American interests in the region during the Cold War era. The Shah was seen as a more favorable leader who would be more receptive to American interests.

On August 19, 1953, military units loyal to Zahedi took control of key government buildings in Tehran while pro-Mossadegh protesters filled the streets. After a day of heavy fighting, Mosaddegh was arrested, tried, and convicted of treason by the Shah's military court. He was later sentenced to three years of jail and placed under house arrest for the remainder of his life. The following day, Shah Mohammad Reza Pahlavi—who had fled Iran during the fighting—returned to Tehran and soon declared martial law. The operation was successful, and Mossadegh was removed from power and replaced with General Zahedi as prime minister.

The operation was carried out by agents from the CIA and British intelligence agency MI6. Specifically, Kermit Roosevelt Jr., the grandson of President Theodore Roosevelt, led the CIA's efforts. He worked closely with Norman Schwarzkopf Sr., whose son, General Schwarzkopf Jr., would later lead US forces in the first Gulf War.

This operation was a primary factor in turning Iranian public opinion against the United States, resulting in the abduction of sixty-six Americans after Iranians overthrew their oppressive, US-installed government. Would these hostages have ever been taken if the United States hadn't interfered in Iranian politics? Probably not.

Cui Bono?

Although Operation Ajax succeeded in removing Mossadegh from power, it ultimately harmed the Iranian people more than it helped them. The new regime led by General Zahedi was oppressive and corrupt. Over time, this led to growing resentment of both Zahedi and the United States among Iranians.

While there were short-term benefits for the United States and Britain, in the long run, neither country benefited from their involvement in Ajax. The short-term benefits included maintaining control over Iran's oil resources and possibly preventing a Communist government from taking power in Iran, which they believed could have potentially spread communism to other countries in the Middle East. In the long term, however, it was Iran's clerical elite and hardline conservative Islamists who benefited most from the overthrow of Mossadegh.

The Shah became increasingly unpopular due to his brutal, repressive regime and pro-Western foreign policies which led to increased political instability in Iran. This eventually resulted in Islamic revolutionaries overthrowing him during the Iranian Revolution in 1979. The Islamic Republic of Iran that emerged after this revolution is an enemy of both the United States and Britain. In addition, Operation Ajax cemented Iranians' suspicion of Western powers and contributed to anti-American sentiment in the country which continues to this day.

The Iranian people were the biggest losers. They lost their freedom, economic stability, and independence and have suffered political and economic upheaval and uncertainty ever since.

Why Does This Matter?

Operation Ajax is significant because it demonstrates how American intervention in other countries can often cause more harm than good. Although some might argue that America's intentions were good—to remove a leader they perceived as being hostile to their interests—the reality is that their actions ultimately led to decades of tension between America and Iran that culminated in one of America's most humiliating foreign policy defeats.

The Iran hostage crisis triggered a long-standing feud between Iran and the United States that continues to this day. In recent years, tensions have ratcheted up once again, with both countries coming close to the brink of war. Here's a timeline of the major events in the forty-four-year history of this complex relationship.

1953: The Coup d'état

The United States led a coup in Iran that toppled the democratically elected government of Prime Minister Mohammad Mossadegh. The United States was concerned about Mossadegh's nationalist policies, which they believed would threaten their access to Iran's oil reserves. The coup installed a government more friendly to their interests under the Shah of Iran, who ruled until he was overthrown in 1979.

1979: The Iran Hostage Crisis Begins

On November 4, 1979, a group of militant Iranian students stormed the US Embassy in Tehran and took sixty-six Americans hostage. The students were angry about the Shah being granted asylum by the US government following his overthrow. They also demanded the return of Iranian assets that had been frozen by the US government.

The hostages were held for 444 days. During that time, they were subjected to psychological and physical abuse by their captors. In response to the crisis, President Jimmy Carter ordered a disastrous rescue mission that ended with eight American servicemen dead and no hostages freed.

1981: US Government Releases Frozen Iranian Assets

In January 1981, shortly before leaving office, President Carter agreed to release over $7 billion in frozen Iranian assets in exchange for the safe release of the hostages.

1995: America Imposes Sanctions on Iran

Responding to Iran's growing nuclear program, as well as the country's support for terrorist organizations, President Bill Clinton issued several executive orders banning US investment in Iran's energy sector as well as banning US trade with and investment in Iran.

2013: Hassan Rouhani Is Elected President

In June 2013, Hassan Rouhani was elected president of Iran after promising to ease tensions with the West and improve the country's struggling economy. His election was seen as a victory for moderates over Iranian hardliners.

2018: Donald Trump Withdraws from Nuclear Deal

After years of negotiations between Iran and world powers, including the United States, an agreement was reached in 2015 to limit Iran's nuclear program in exchange for the lifting of international sanctions. But in May 2018, President Donald Trump withdrew from the deal—overruling objections from European allies who had worked hard to broker it—and reimposed sanctions on Iran.

2019: Tensions Begin Escalating Again

In June 2019, Trump came close to ordering an airstrike on Iranian targets in response to Iran shooting down a US spy drone; Trump aborted the strike at the last minute because it would have killed over a hundred people. Then in January 2020, a drone strike ordered by Trump killed Iranian Gen. Qassem Soleimani—one of the country's most powerful military leaders—near Baghdad International Airport.

The United States enjoyed a peaceful relationship with Iran until the coup of 1953. Since then, relations have been strained with distrust and meddling bringing the two countries close to armed conflict. If Western governments have meddled to this extent in one country, it is probable that similar endeavors take place all across the globe, with many foreign governments trying to manipulate world politics.

What We Learned

1. The story of "who started it" is often not accurate. Some people still believe that the hostage crisis of 1979 was an unprovoked act of aggression upon the United States—they are unaware that from the perspective of the Iranians, they were taking revenge on the United States for overthrowing their elected government, replacing it with one that would better serve Western interests, and supporting the Shah even after they removed him from power.

2. "Blowback" is real. The repercussions of international meddling or violence may take years or even decades to be felt, but people rarely forgive or forget when they feel their country has been attacked by a foreign power.

3. Actions by the government or the military can have harmful consequences for innocent civilians; it's often the poorest people who suffer from the machinations of those in power.

4. International meddling by the government for political or financial gain often causes harm to the people living in that country. The people of Iran were subjected to harsh governance under the Shah, even though they had elected a leader they trusted who they thought treated them well.

Declassified Details of Iranian Coup

A Report from *Foreign Policy* magazine

August 18, 1953

In early 1951, amid great popular acclaim, [Iranian Prime Minister Muhammad] Mossadegh nationalized Iran's oil industry. A fuming United Kingdom began conspiring with U.S. intelligence services to overthrow Mossadegh and restore the monarchy under the shah. (Though some in the U.S. State Department, the newly released cables show, blamed British intransigence for the tensions and sought to work with Mossadegh.)

The coup attempt began on August 15 but was swiftly thwarted. Mossadegh made dozens of arrests. Gen. Fazlollah Zahedi, a top conspirator, went into hiding, and the shah fled the country.

The CIA, believing the coup to have failed, called it off.

"Operation has been tried and failed and we should not participate in any operation against Mossadegh which could be traced back to US," CIA headquarters wrote to its station chief in Iran in a newly declassified cable sent on Aug. 18, 1953. "Operations against Mossadegh should be discontinued."

That is the cable which Kermit Roosevelt, top CIA officer in Iran, purportedly and famously ignored, according to Malcolm Byrne, who directs the U.S.-Iran Relations Project at the National Security Archive at George Washington University.

At least "one guy was in the room with Kermit Roosevelt when he got this cable," Byrne told Foreign Policy. "[Roosevelt] said no — we're not done here." It was already known that Roosevelt had not carried out an order from Langley to cease and desist. But the cable itself and its contents were not previously published.

The consequences of his decision were momentous. The next day, on August 19, 1953, with the aid of "rented" crowds widely believed to have been arranged with CIA assistance, the coup succeeded.

Iran's nationalist hero was jailed, the monarchy restored under the Western-friendly shah, and Anglo-Iranian oil — renamed British Petroleum — tried to get its fields back. (But didn't really: Despite the coup, nationalist pushback against a return to foreign control of oil was too much, leaving BP and other majors to share Iran's oil wealth with Tehran.)

The U.S government long denied involvement in the coup. The State Department first released coup-related documents in 1989, but edited out any reference to CIA involvement. Public outrage coaxed a government promise to release a more complete edition, and some material came out in 2013.

Two years later, the full installment of declassified material was scheduled—but might have interfered with Iran nuclear talks and were delayed again, Byrne said. They were finally released last week, though numerous original CIA telegrams from that period are known to have disappeared or been destroyed long ago.

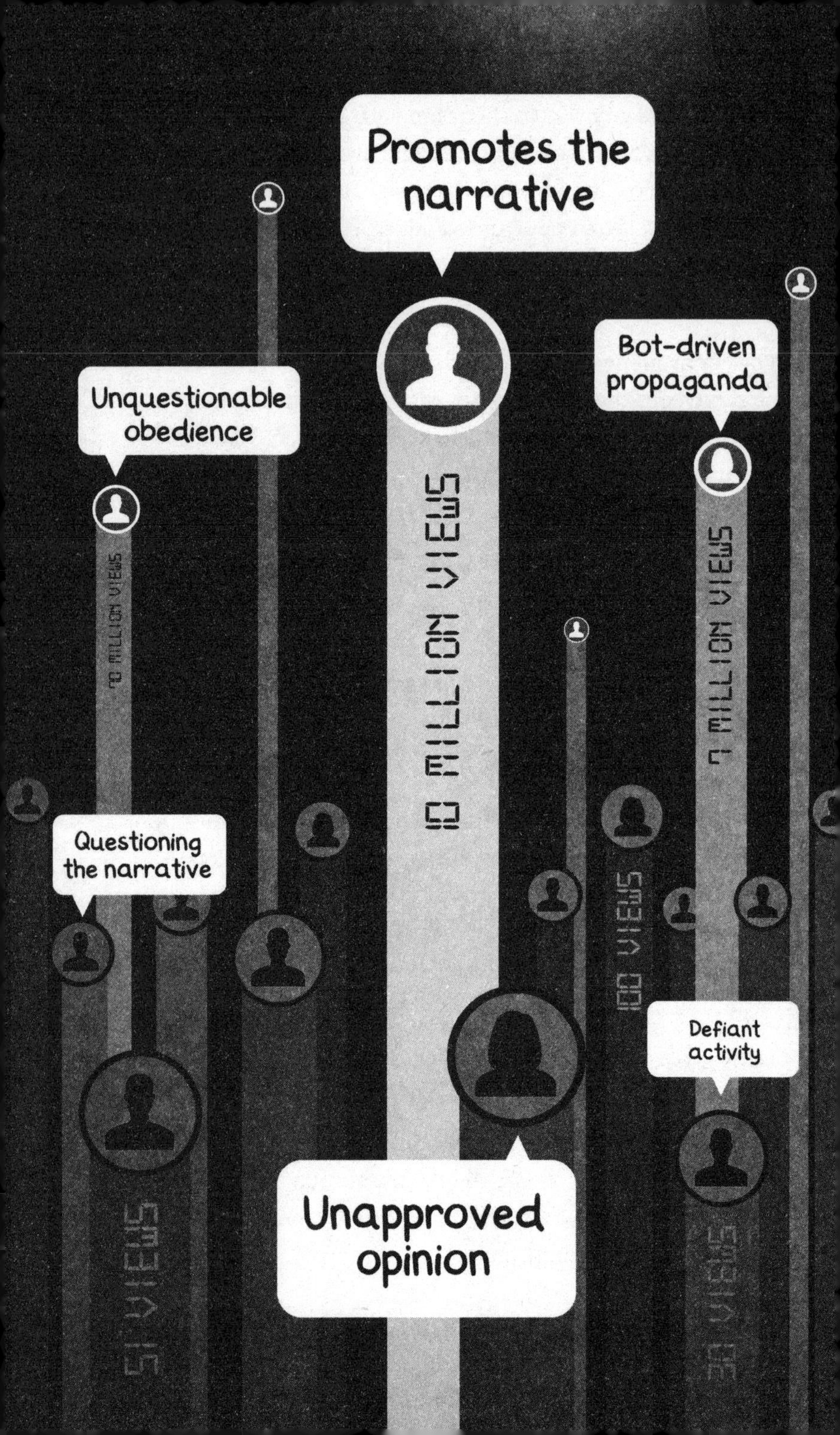
Promotes the narrative
Unquestionable obedience
Bot-driven propaganda
10 MILLION VIEWS
7 MILLION VIEWS
100 VIEWS
Questioning the narrative
Defiant activity
Unapproved opinion

Social Media
MANIPULATION

Social media platforms have become battlegrounds for hidden agendas, as governments exploit the power of manipulation.

If you're a teenager, there's a good chance you use social media. You might be on Facebook, Twitter, Instagram, TikTok, Snapchat, or any number of other platforms. And while social media can be a lot of fun, it can also be used for more serious purposes.

For example, did you know that the US government has used social media to influence public opinion in other countries? It's true! In 2006, the US government launched a program called Operation Earnest Voice, which was designed to use social media to counter negative narratives about the United States in foreign countries and to protect Americans from harm.

The operation made use of fake accounts on social media platforms like Facebook and Twitter to spread pro-American messages. These messages were designed to combat negative stereotypes about the United States and its people.

For example, many people in foreign countries believe that all Americans are wealthy and have easy lives. The goal of Earnest Voice was to show that not all Americans are wealthy and that life in the United States is not always easy.

In addition to spreading sympathetic messages about the United States, the operation also aimed to counter the messaging of terrorist organizations like ISIS. For example, ISIS often uses social media to recruit new members and promote its radical ideology. By using social media to spread positive messages about the United States, Earnest Voice hoped to make potential recruits think twice before joining ISIS or other terrorist organizations. It helped protect people in the United States from extremists.

Things Aren't Always What They Seem

Operation Earnest Voice was one of the first attempts by the US military to use social media for propaganda purposes. The operation was run by the US Special Operations Command and involved creating fake accounts on social media sites like MySpace and Facebook to spread pro-American messages. The accounts would then be used to "friend" or follow real users in order to send them messages containing links to pro-American websites or videos. This was an attempt to sway the conversation about the war in Iraq and Afghanistan. In some cases, the fake accounts would also leave comments on users' profiles in an attempt to sway public opinion.

The government knew studies show people are more likely to believe messages that come from people they know or trust, so they built a program around building a sense of trust and community with people around the world, thus making it easier to spread information and influence the masses.

The goal of the operation was to influence public opinion about US foreign policy, particularly in countries that were hostile or resistant to US efforts. The program was reportedly successful in some cases, but its full success and reach remains unknown. The operation worked through "traditional media, as well as via Web sites and regional public-affairs blogging" to amplify "moderate voices" more favorable to the US government's position.

While the program was not illegal, it has been heavily criticized by some who say that it violates international law and basic principles of free speech. Critics have also raised concerns about how much control the US government has over citizens' online conversations.

Earnest Voice raises important questions about the use of digital platforms by governments to influence public opinion and shape international relations. It also highlights how easy it is for governments to manipulate information and data on a massive scale. And it makes you wonder, is a system like this—designed for foreign influence during a time of war—susceptible to being turned inward on the American people to influence *them*?

Governments that develop powerful surveillance and communication technologies are often tempted to begin using these tools to control their own citizens, and that has certainly been the case with social media. And because these platforms reach so many people, they create an opportunity for politicians to influence others. During COVID-19, for example, the Biden administration exerted pressure on social media companies to suppress people and their opinions that challenged the narrative they preferred—knowing that by depriving people of seeing certain content on social media they could alter what those people know and how they act.

Do we as citizens have the right to be free from propaganda efforts by our own government? Is it okay for the government to monitor or influence our social media activity without our knowledge or consent? Is it okay for the government to use programs developed for use against potential enemies on their own populations?

Cui Bono?

By using social media, Earnest Voice sought to shape public opinion on global issues like terrorism and democracy. The target audience of this campaign were (initially, at least) foreign audiences, particularly those in Islamic countries. The US and its allies viewed Earnest Voice as a form of public diplomacy, using persuasive methods to influence public opinion in areas of concern for the United States. It was a way to hopefully save American lives.

The primary beneficiaries of Earnest Voice were the US government and its allies. By attempting to shape public opinion abroad, the United States hoped to improve its image in countries with whom it has strained diplomatic relations. Additionally, by using social media to reach large numbers of people quickly and effectively, the United States was able to spread its message more effectively than through traditional means such as press releases or TV commercials.

Information control and persuasion using systems like Earnest Voice—or simply putting political pressure on social media companies to do the government's bidding—can be very beneficial for those in power as it enables them to shape the narrative about how citizens perceive reality. If they can be duped into believing or acting differently, that enables those who control the propaganda to exert control and achieve their outcomes, instead of letting people with free will independently decide.

Why Does This Matter?

Online propaganda is any type of communication—images, videos, articles, etc.—that is used to influence or control a large group of people. This type of propaganda is often used by governments to control their citizens by disseminating biased or false information. And while it starts with a more noble intent—such as influencing people in foreign countries hostile to our own—these systems become tempting for those in power to use on their own people.

There are a few reasons why online propaganda matters. First, it can be used to spread dangerous misinformation. For example, if the government is trying to cover up a scandal, they may use propaganda to discredit anyone who shares information about it. Second, online propaganda can be used to stifle dissent and silence minority groups. For example, if the government wants to prevent its citizens from speaking out against them, they may use propaganda to make people afraid to speak up. Finally, online propaganda can have a real impact on people's lives. For example, if the government is trying to promote a certain agenda they may use propaganda to try to convince people that it is in their best interest to support that agenda.

With the discovery of the US government's actions related to Earnest Voice, it becomes clear that if the government has the technology and manpower to use online manipulation and propaganda to change the way people in foreign countries see their own country and their own government, we should not be surprised when they use that technology on Americans as well.

What We Learned

1. The government will spy on and manipulate their own citizens using the same programs and tactics that they use against their enemies.

2. The government interferes in the social media lives of citizens of other countries in an attempt to trick them into being influenced by ideas that favor a different agenda.

3. It is relatively easy for a person to create a fake online persona—carefully crafting an online image and building relationships with people who don't know that they aren't who they say they are.

4. People who are targets of a secret US operation don't always know they were targeted, even after the program has been exposed publicly.

5. Tools created by the government for use against foreign individuals can easily be turned inward on its own citizens for political control.

Revealed: US spy operation that manipulates social media

An investigative report from *The Guardian*

March 17, 2011

The US military is developing software that will let it secretly manipulate social media sites by using fake online personas to influence internet conversations and spread pro-American propaganda.

A Californian corporation has been awarded a contract with United States Central Command (Centcom), which oversees US armed operations in the Middle East and Central Asia, to develop what is described as an "online persona management service" that will allow one US serviceman or woman to control up to 10 separate identities based all over the world.

The project has been likened by web experts to China's attempts to control and restrict free speech on the internet. Critics are likely to complain that it will allow the US military to create a false consensus in online conversations, crowd out unwelcome opinions and smother commentaries or reports that do not correspond with its own objectives.

The discovery that the US military is developing false online personalities—known to users of social media as "sock puppets"—could also encourage other governments, private companies and non-government organisations to do the same.

The Centcom contract stipulates that each fake online persona must have a convincing background, history and supporting details, and that up to 50 US-based controllers should be able to operate false identities from their workstations "without fear of being discovered by sophisticated adversaries."

Centcom spokesman Commander Bill Speaks said: "The technology supports classified blogging activities on foreign-language websites to enable Centcom to counter violent extremist and enemy propaganda outside the US."

Centcom's contract requires for each controller the provision of one "virtual private server" located in the United States and others appearing to be outside the US to give the impression the fake personas are real people located in different parts of the world.

It also calls for "traffic mixing," blending the persona controllers' internet usage with the usage of people outside Centcom in a manner that must offer "excellent cover and powerful deniability."

The multiple persona contract is thought to have been awarded as part of a programme called Operation Earnest Voice (OEV), which was first developed in Iraq as a psychological warfare weapon against the online presence of al-Qaida supporters and others ranged against coalition forces. Since then, OEV is reported to have expanded into a $200m programme and is thought to have been used against jihadists across Pakistan, Afghanistan and the Middle East.

OEV is seen by senior US commanders as a vital counter-terrorism and counter-radicalisation programme. In evidence to the US Senate's armed services committee last year, General David Petraeus, then commander of Centcom, described the operation as an effort to "counter extremist ideology and propaganda and to ensure that credible voices in the region are heard." He said the US military's objective was to be "first with the truth."

FEDERAL GOVERNMENT
Happy anniversary, darling!
Until death do us part!
Heh, got that right...

Poisoned BOOZE

Good intentions and dire consequences collided during Prohibition when anti-alcohol crusaders poisoned the product, leading to thousands of hospitalizations and deaths.

In the early nineteenth century, many Americans crusaded against alcohol. The Temperance Movement, as it was called, promoted the prohibition of alcohol and wanted the government to make its use illegal.

In the decades following, many organizations formed and joined together to push for prohibition—the Women's Christian Temperance Union, the Prohibition Party, and the Anti-Saloon League. And in 1919, these groups got what they had been fighting for—an amendment to the US Constitution that prohibited the manufacture, sale, and transportation of alcoholic beverages. Then Congress passed the Volstead Act to enforce the new amendment and punish those who broke the new law.

Prohibition laws were now in force, but there were widespread violations of the law. There were individuals who broke the law to produce, smuggle, and sell alcoholic beverages. These people were often called bootleggers, since they would often hide flasks of liquor in their boots to evade detection by government officials. There were also secret bars or clubs, called speakeasies, that sold alcohol illegally to customers. They were often hidden behind unmarked doors inside an otherwise ordinary building—and they often were protected because their owners bribed the local police and politicians. Then there were organized crime syndicates that turned the distribution of illegal alcohol into an industry. Al Capone, and others like him, became famous for building large criminal organizations that profited off of this black-market product.

Advocates of Prohibition had gotten their victory—the law had been changed—but they wanted to see it actually enforced. They wanted to see fewer people drink alcohol.

They wanted to see people give up drinking it. So one group of Prohibition supporters devised a plan to begin poisoning the nation's alcohol supply, so that people drinking the illegal alcohol would get sick and possibly die. It was a controversial proposal from this group, and it definitely had an impact.

New York City was an epicenter of illegal booze production and distribution. And Charles Norris was the city's first medical examiner and a witness to this group's poisoning scheme. In December 1926, Norris saw dozens of deaths in his city alone, and many more incapacitated in the hospital, as a result of drinking hazardous chemicals contaminating the bootlegged booze. As New Yorkers continued to die, Norris decided to speak out. The group that was poisoning alcohol "knows it is not stopping drinking," he said. "It knows what bootleggers are doing with it and yet it continues its poisoning processes, heedless of the fact that people determined to drink are daily absorbing that poison."

Things Aren't Always What They Seem

Who was this group of advocates poisoning alcohol? It was the US government.

Throughout the Prohibition era, grain alcohol and liquor were difficult for people to get, so they turned to other alcohols found in things like paint thinner and wood polish. This "industrial alcohol" was essentially grain alcohol but with chemicals added to it in a process called "denaturing," making it undrinkable. But when the government banned booze, it created an incentive for bootleggers to "renature" that cheap alcohol to make it drinkable again so they could turn a profit in a black market.

Congress had put the US Treasury Department in charge of enforcing the Prohibition laws. They estimated that over 60 million gallons of industrial alcohol were stolen by bootleggers looking to convert it into a drinkable beverage. So in late 1926, when Norris started seeing all the poisoning deaths, the government modified the denaturing formulas to double the amount of poisonous chemicals present. They included methanol, an alcohol that is toxic to humans. They also used things like soap, formaldehyde, sulfuric acid, or iodine. The president of the Anti-Saloon League was very supportive, since after the law passed, drinking rates did not decrease. He argued that if people broke the law and drank poisoned alcohol, it was their own fault. "The Government is under no obligation to furnish the people with alcohol that is drinkable when the Constitution prohibits it. The person who drinks this industrial alcohol is a deliberate suicide," he said.

Not everybody who drank the renatured-but-poisoned alcohol died. The chemicals induced vomiting, hallucinations, and blindness; many people were sick. But countless others died, and Norris looked around at the poisoned bodies of those in New York City. "They are definitely dead and there is no doubt as to the cause of their death," he wrote. "These are not statistics, but the bare record of a tragedy as shocking and in a sense dramatic as a fearful crash on the subway." And yet the government continued to poison the alcohol supply, knowing that this was the result. By the time the Prohibition laws were finally repealed a few years later, around 10,000 people had died by being poisoned by their own government.

Cui Bono?

When the government bans something, that doesn't magically make that thing disappear. Instead, it creates a black market where people continue to buy, sell, and use the banned item—but now it's far more costly and dangerous to do so. There is a lot of risk from getting caught, so everything is pushed into the shadows where people can avoid detection. And criminals love when things are prohibited, because it allows them to profit due to decreased competition. Just like today's cartels financially benefit because certain drugs they produce are banned by the government, bootleggers and gangsters like Al Capone benefited by what the government did during Prohibition.

But the rise of these criminals was a natural reaction to what others were doing—the prohibitionists, who wanted to make alcohol illegal, thinking that would lead fewer people to drink. The prohibitionists benefited from the law—and from the government's controversial efforts to enforce it, such as with this poisoning—because the efforts increased their influence, raised funds for their organizations, and punished others for doing something they thought was bad.

For these people, the deaths were but a mere stumbling block on the path to victory. The president of the Anti-Saloon League said that "To root out a bad habit costs many lives and long years of effort," almost suggesting that these poison deaths were a sacrifice on the altar of Prohibition. And one of the government officials in charge of the poisoning efforts said that if the result of thousands of Americans dying from poisoned booze was a country where fewer people drank alcohol, then "a good job will have been done."

Why Does This Matter?

While the subject is controversial for some, the reality is that today there is a different kind of prohibition in place—on drugs, where cartels profit, and many people continue using these substances despite it being illegal. And while the "war on drugs" has failed just as badly as Prohibition did, many in the government are okay with the carnage because they feel like it's an acceptable byproduct on the journey towards stopping people from consuming bad things.

As a result of this war, many people have been hurt or killed. Countless people have been put in jail or prison for possessing or using drugs without hurting anyone else. They've lost their jobs, their rights to own a firearm for self-defense, their parental rights, and more. While some choices adults make aren't healthy or helpful, that doesn't necessarily mean there should be a law to punish people for those choices.

It's clear from history that simply prohibiting people from doing something won't solve the underlying problem; people will continue to use things that they desire, but when they have to go to the black market to do so, the risk increases and so does the harm and death.

The government's policies today are perhaps not as controversial as they were in the early 1900s when they were directly involved in introducing poison into the nation's alcohol supply, but the effects of these policies are no less harmful. While it is appropriate to advocate for others to stop consuming certain substances, it is improper—and ineffective—to involve the government and make it a crime. History shows that this doesn't work, yet that lesson seems to be one that very few government officials are willing to learn. Instead, they continue repeating the mistakes of the past—and thousands of people are forced to suffer as a result.

What We Learned

1. Good intentions are often used to build support for controversial practices. It's important to look not just at the intentions of a particular politician or program, but at the effect their proposal would cause—including unintended consequences.

2. To many people, the ends justify the means—those who wanted others to stop drinking alcohol were content with the government killing some of them if it meant achieving their goals.

3. Prohibiting people from engaging in an activity doesn't mean they will all stop that activity—it just pushes people into a black market where costs go up and danger increases. The government turns law-abiding citizens into criminals overnight.

Prohibition Regulations

A memo from the Treasury Department to Collectors of Internal Revenue and Prohibition Administrators

October 8, 1926

Effective January 1, 1927, completely denatured alcohol, formula No. 5, will be compounded according to either one of the following formulas:

After April 1, 1927, it will be compounded only according to the first one of the stated formulas.

OPTION 1

>100 parts by volume, ethyl alcohol, not less than 1600 proof.
>
>4 parts by volume approved methanol (denaturing grade).
>
>0.75 parts by volume of the compound or one similar thereto known as aldehol grade A.
>
>0.5 parts by volume approved benzine (kerosene).

OPTION 2

>100 parts by volume ethyl alcohol, not less than 1600 proof.
>
>4 parts by volume approved methanol (denaturing grade).
>
>0.25 parts by volume approved pyridine bases.
>
>0.5 parts by volume approved benzine (kerosene).

Specifications for aldehol grade A, or compounds similar thereto.— A product of the oxidation of kerosene having the following characteristics:

*Specific graivity.—*Not over 0.825 at 60° F.

*Distillation range.—*When 100 cubic centimeters are subjected to distillation in the same manner and apparatus specified for determining the boiling point of methanol, not less than 20 cubic centimeters will distill over under 200° C. and not less than 95 cubic centimeters will distill over under 290° C.

*Behavior with Schiff's reagent (aldehydes).—*Ten cubic centimeters of the liquid with 15 cubic centimeters of Schiff's reagent must show decided violet color within 30 seconds after addition and agitation.

*Solubility in 90 per cent ethyl alcohol.—*When 10 cubic centimeters of the liquid is placed in a stoppered cylinder, graduated to one-tenth of a cubic centimeter, an equal quantity of 90 per cent ethyl alcohol added, and the contents shaken and allowed to stand, the alcohol layer will measure not less than 12 cubic centimeters.

*Iodine number.—*The iodine number shall be not less than 35.

The sample submitted for approval shall have the characteristic odor and color of the standard sample sent to the authorized chemist.

D. H. BLAIR, Commissioner of Internal Revenue.
A. W. MELLON, Secretary of the Treasury.

Director Clapper, is the US government illegally collecting the private online data of American citizens?
Uhh... no?
CONGRESS
FIBBARATOR
LIAR.LIAR.LIAR.
INITIATING PANTS-ON-FIRE SEQUENCE.

Unconstitutional
SURVEILLANCE

In the wake of 9/11, the federal government created a massive network of surveillance systems to spy on innocent people—and then lied to the American people about it.

The Washington Post

FRIDAY, JUNE 7, 2013

U.S. mines Internet firms' data, documents show

Google, Facebook, Apple, Yahoo deny giving NSA direct access to servers

BY BARTON GELLMAN AND LAURA POITRAS

Agency knows much about public, but we know little about it

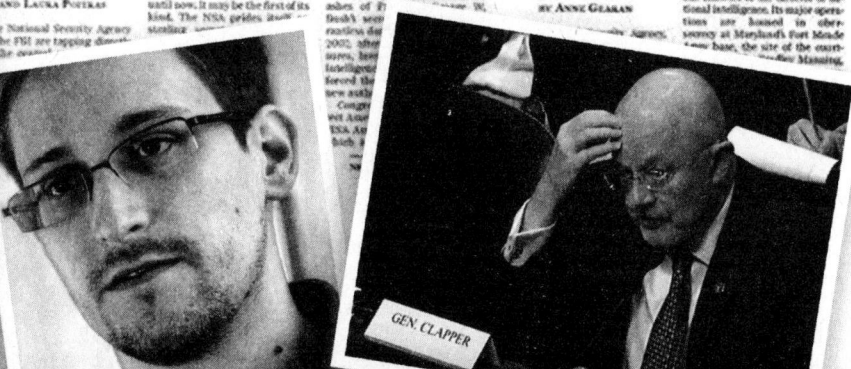

BY ANNE GEARAN

Picture this: You're at home, scrolling social media or doing some online research. Unbeknownst to you, someone's watching. Someone's always watching. It's not a creepy neighbor or a nosy relative—it's your own government. Unsettling, isn't it?

For years, this scenario was nothing more than a story whispered in hushed tones in the darker corners of the internet. It was a "conspiracy theory"—the kind that's dismissed with a wave of the hand and a roll of the eyes. The idea that the government was keeping tabs on its own citizens—spying on them without their knowledge or consent—was seen as an absurd speculation that belonged to dystopian novels and high-octane Hollywood blockbusters. Not something that could be happening in real life, right?

But if history has taught us anything, it's that reality often surpasses fiction. And the line between paranoia and legitimate concern is thinner than we'd like to think—especially when it comes to the delicate matter of privacy and surveillance.

The whispers grew louder, slowly but steadily. Privacy advocates and concerned citizens believed it was likely that the government was surveilling its own populace. But there was a problem: there was no concrete proof—just suspicion and fear. The government was silent, unwilling to appease the conspiracy theories and reveal any of its secrets. So the whispers remained whispers, and the status quo remained unchallenged. At least for a while.

But as it often happens, the truth has a funny way of making itself heard. And when it does, it's usually louder, harsher, and more shocking than we could ever imagine.

Things Aren't Always What They Seem

Some people knew that the conspiracy theories were true, including members of the Senate Intelligence Committee—members of Congress who were given access to top secret information about the government's activities. Senator Ron Wyden was on this committee, and he was concerned about the surveillance programs the government was operating. In March 2013, Wyden asked Director of National Intelligence James Clapper whether the US government was collecting "any type of data at all on millions or hundreds of millions of Americans."

Let's pause and consider the question. Senator Wyden knew the answer to the question he was asking. His purpose was not to figure out something he didn't know; he had access to top secret information and knew what the government was doing. He also knew that the public didn't know, and that if they did, it would be a scandal. So his purpose was to force Clapper into an awkward situation. If Clapper said yes, then there would be national outrage and news headlines galore. If he said no, then he would be lying to the public and perpetuating a government conspiracy. Senator Wyden also gave Clapper advance notice of the question, so he certainly wasn't caught off guard.

Was the government collecting *any* type of data at all on Americans? Clapper responded: "No, sir. ... Not wittingly." He lied.

For a moment, the idea of widespread government surveillance was pushed back into the corners of society—the playground of conspiracy theorists and crazy people.

But as the American public was reassured by the head of "intelligence" that nothing sinister was afoot, one of the viewers watching Clapper's interview knew otherwise. His name: Edward Snowden.

A former CIA employee and NSA contractor, Snowden had spent years operating in the complex web of American intelligence, and he had seen things—things that contradicted the official narrative. Things that painted a picture of a surveillance apparatus far more intrusive and far-reaching than anyone could imagine. He had direct access to documents that proved Clapper had lied to the public, and he himself had observed programs and tools that allowed government employees to spy on any American citizen.

Outraged by Clapper's lie, Snowden decided to do what few others have been brave enough to do. He became a whistleblower, sending these secret documents to journalists who used them as evidence to publish articles revealing the truth about what the government was doing—and how Clapper had completely lied to cover up the government's conspiracy.

Snowden's leaks revealed that the NSA was indeed engaged in mass surveillance programs, both domestic and international. Far from being a targeted operation against suspects of terrorism, it was a dragnet that scooped up millions of innocent people's communication data. They had access to phone records, emails, and even the ability to tap into the central servers of nine prominent US internet companies.

One of the most controversial programs, codenamed PRISM, allowed the NSA to extract audio and video chats, photographs, emails, documents, and connection logs that enabled analysts to track people. It was a blatant contradiction of Clapper's earlier denial. The truth was out: the government had been spying on its citizens, and they had lied about it.

Cui Bono?

Who stands to gain from such a massive surveillance scheme? Who was benefiting from keeping this a secret from the public? In truth, there are quite a few "winners" in this scenario, and their gain comes at the expense of ordinary people's privacy and civil liberties.

Firstly, there's the US government itself. With access to unprecedented amounts of information, it has an extraordinary ability to keep tabs on not just potential threats, but ordinary citizens as well. Whether it is investigating criminal activity, assessing public sentiment, or monitoring individuals of interest, this dragnet surveillance capability offers a sweeping view of the nation's pulse. The more data it can gather, the more power it can wield. We can see this in China where the government monitors people's actions and behaviors. They have a social credit score program that uses that vast amount of data to punish anyone acting in ways the government doesn't like. This allows the government to more easily control its people.

This surveillance also has a significant political aspect. With such a large amount of information, those in power can potentially exploit it for political gain. Be it opposition research, character assassination, or even blackmail, the potential for abuse is tremendous. This is not to say that it has necessarily occurred (though it probably has), but the possibility is certainly there, creating a worrying dimension of potential political manipulation.

Next, we should consider the intelligence community. These are the folks who spend their lives trying to piece together puzzles to protect national security. For them, more data usually means more opportunities to connect the dots. From their perspective, these surveillance programs could be seen as invaluable tools in their work, helping them to uncover threats and protect the nation. Typically, people in this position justify tools like this because it can make their job easier and allow them to catch more bad guys more quickly. To them, the ends (going after criminals) justifies the means (spying on innocent people). The climate of secrecy also protects the intelligence community from scrutiny and criticism. With the operations hidden behind a veil of national security, they can deflect questions, avoid accountability, and operate with relative impunity.

Then there are the corporations, especially those in the defense and technology sectors. Companies contracted by the government for surveillance-related work see their profits skyrocket. They build the infrastructure, develop the hardware, and maintain the systems and software that make this mass surveillance possible. In essence, they are paid handsomely to help the government spy on people. This creates a symbiotic relationship, with both parties benefiting from the continuation and expansion of these programs.

Finally, we must consider the broader implications in the global arena. The NSA's far-reaching surveillance offers the

United States an advantage in geopolitical power struggles. It can spy on foreign governments, global institutions, corporations, and individuals, thereby gaining insights, predicting moves, and influencing outcomes to its favor. In the world of international relations, knowledge is power, and the NSA's capabilities make the United States a formidable player.

Why Does This Matter?

If we have nothing to hide, then we shouldn't be bothered by our government conducting surveillance on us... right? Wrong!

First, let's talk about the Fourth Amendment to the US Constitution. This is a part of the Bill of Rights that was crafted by the Founding Fathers to address abuses they themselves faced from the British, specifically the infamous "writs of assistance." These were broad search warrants that allowed British officials to search anyone, anytime, for any reason—or even for no reason at all. The colonists were deeply troubled by this, and their experiences led to the creation of the Fourth Amendment, which states that "The right of the people to be secure in their persons, houses, papers, and effects, against unreasonable searches and seizures, shall not be violated."

One critical aspect of the Fourth Amendment is the requirement of particularity. This means that in order for the government to conduct a search, it must have a specific target and a specific reason. You can't just go on a fishing expedition hoping to catch a criminal—you need to have a reasonable suspicion that a specific individual is involved in criminal activity. In other words, you need a warrant, and that warrant must "particularly describ[e] the place to be searched, and the persons or things to be seized." This focus on the individual is a key aspect of our constitutional protections against government overreach.

Now, consider the NSA's mass surveillance programs in light of this requirement. They are, in essence, the digital equivalent of those hated writs of assistance. Rather than targeting specific individuals based on reasonable suspicion, these programs sweep up the communications of millions of innocent people, hoping to find a needle in a haystack. This is the very definition of a general warrant— the very thing the Fourth Amendment was designed to prohibit. This means that these surveillance programs are unconstitutional.

Now, back to the claim that if we have nothing to hide, then we shouldn't care about our privacy being invaded. On the surface, this might make a little sense. After all, if we're living upright lives, why would we care if the government sees our emails or listens to our phone calls? But this argument is deeply flawed. Privacy is a fundamental aspect of a free society. It's not just about hiding bad things—it's about having control over our own lives, our own thoughts, and our own experiences.

We have a right to be left alone, to be free from unwarranted intrusion, and to have a space where we can be ourselves without fear of judgment or reprisal. And even if we're living angelic lives, that doesn't mean we're safe from harm. There are countless obscure crimes and regulations that we might unknowingly violate. If the government has access to every detail of our lives, it's not hard to imagine a situation where someone could use this information to manipulate or prosecute us.

And consider this: a society in which the government has access to every detail of every citizen's life is a society ripe for abuse. If they can monitor us constantly, what's to stop them from using that power to silence dissent, to manipulate public opinion, or to persecute people? The danger these privacy programs present isn't just a threat to individuals—it's a threat to how our society is structured.

So, why does this matter? It matters because our rights, our freedoms, and our very way of life are at stake. It matters because the government has been secretly spying on its own people, violating the Constitution, and lying about it. It matters because even after the Snowden revelations, the surveillance continues. It matters because if they've been doing this in secret, who knows what else they might be up to?

This isn't just about emails and phone calls. This is about the kind of society we want to live in. Do we want to live in a surveillance state, where every move is monitored and privacy is a thing of the past? Or do we want to live in a free society, where our rights are respected and our government is held accountable? We need to answer those questions and then do something about it.

A government that acts in secret, outside its constitutionally enumerated powers, and shielded from the oversight of elected officials, is, simply put, a subversive gang of criminals—in other words a conspiracy.

What We Learned

1. The NSA's mass surveillance programs directly violate the Fourth Amendment to the US Constitution. This amendment, crafted to protect us from unreasonable searches and seizures, requires particularity—specific targets and reasons for searches. Mass surveillance programs do not meet this requirement, as they collect data on millions of innocent people indiscriminately.

2. The idea that "If you've got nothing to hide, you've got nothing to worry about" fails to recognize the value of privacy in a free society. Privacy isn't about hiding wrongdoing—it's about the right to control personal information and live without unwarranted intrusion.

3. With the power to monitor everyone, the government could potentially use this information to pressure, manipulate, or even punish people for obscure violations. It's happening in China, and it can happen in the United States too.

4. The government has not only been conducting unconstitutional surveillance but has also lied about it. Even after Edward Snowden's revelations, the surveillance continues. This raises questions about other potential covert operations and underscores the need for government transparency and accountability.

Millions of People Tracked

An excerpt of an article from *The Guardian*

September 30, 2013

The National Security Agency is storing the online metadata of millions of internet users for up to a year, regardless of whether or not they are persons of interest to the agency, top secret documents reveal.

Metadata provides a record of almost anything a user does online, from browsing history — such as map searches and websites visited – to account details, email activity, and even some account passwords. This can be used to build a detailed picture of an individual's life.

The Obama administration has repeatedly stated that the NSA keeps only the content of messages and communications of people it is intentionally targeting — but internal documents reveal the agency retains vast amounts of metadata.

An introductory guide to digital network intelligence for NSA field agents, included in documents disclosed by former contractor Edward Snowden, describes the agency's metadata repository, codenamed Marina. Any computer metadata picked up by NSA collection systems is routed to the Marina database, the guide explains. Phone metadata is sent to a separate system.

"The Marina metadata application tracks a user's browser experience, gathers contact information/content and develops summaries of target," the analysts' guide explains. "This tool offers the ability to export the data in a variety of formats, as well as create various charts to assist in pattern-of-life development."

The guide goes on to explain Marina's unique capability: "Of the more distinguishing features, Marina has the ability to look back on the last 365 days' worth of DNI metadata seen by the Sigint collection system, **regardless** whether or not it was tasked for collection." [Emphasis in original.]

On Saturday, the *New York Times* reported that the NSA was using its metadata troves to build profiles of US citizens' social connections, associations and in some cases location, augmenting the material the agency collects with additional information bought in from the commercial sector, which is is not subject to the same legal restrictions as other data.

The ability to look back on a full year's history for any individual whose data was collected — either deliberately or incidentally — offers the NSA the potential to find information on people who have later become targets. But it relies on storing the personal data of large numbers of internet users who are not, and never will be, of interest to the US intelligence community.

Marina aggregates NSA metadata from an array of sources, some targeted, others on a large scale. Programs such as Prism — which operates through legally compelled "partnerships" with major internet companies — allow the NSA to obtain content and metadata on thousands of targets without individual warrants.

The NSA also collects enormous quantities of metadata from the fibre-optic cables that make up the backbone of the internet. The agency has placed taps on undersea cables, and is given access to internet data through partnerships with American telecoms companies.

TARGET:
MARTIN LUTHER
KING, JR.
TARGET:
MALCOLM X
TARGET:
CASSIUS CLAY
AKA: MUHAMMAD ALI

COINTELPRO

In their pursuit of justice, activists encountered a hidden adversary—covert government surveillance and manipulation. These clandestine programs aimed to suppress dissent and preserve the existing power structure.

Picture this: It's the 1960s. The Civil Rights Movement is in full swing, and at its helm is a charismatic leader, Martin Luther King Jr. His powerful speeches and peaceful protests are inspiring a wave of change across America. The echoes of "I have a dream" still linger in the air, uniting people in their quest for equality.

Now, imagine you're Martin Luther King Jr. himself. You're trying to change the world, to fight for justice and equality, but there's a constant feeling of unease. You notice you're being followed. There are unfamiliar faces at your rallies, listening a little too attentively.

You discover that your phone calls are being tapped and personal letters intercepted. Someone is spying on you, and it's not just some rogue racists or disgruntled individuals. It's organized and relentless.

And it's not just surveillance. They're trying to discredit you, planting false stories in the media. They're turning your friends against you, causing divisions within your organization. They even send you a letter, suggesting you should take your own life.

Your home, your privacy, your personal life—nothing is off limits. The threat is real, constant, and ever-growing.

You then learn that this same organized group is similarly surveilling some of your friends and associates—people whose political views are a threat to this group. As you grow in prominence, the attacks continue and increase, all in an effort to undermine your work.

Things Aren't Always What They Seem

This all happened to King and many others, and the organized group targeting them was their own government—specifically, the Federal Bureau of Investigation.

The covert project was named COINTELPRO, short for Counter Intelligence Program. It was a secret FBI program created in 1956 to "expose, disrupt, misdirect, discredit, or otherwise neutralize" the activities of individuals and organizations the FBI considered subversive. Yes, those are the actual words from the official documents.

To "neutralize" King, the FBI resorted to an arsenal of underhanded tactics. They sent him an anonymous letter, known now as the "suicide letter," suggesting he kill himself. They bugged his hotel rooms, hoping to uncover salacious details to ruin his reputation. And it wasn't just King. His family, friends, and associates were all subject to this unwarranted and insidious invasion of privacy.

But King wasn't the only target. COINTELPRO also aimed its shadowy operations at the Southern Christian Leadership Conference, the Student Nonviolent Coordinating Committee, the Black Panther Party, and anti-Vietnam War activists. Even harmless groups promoting racial and gender equality found themselves on the FBI's hit list. Anyone who posed a perceived threat to the status quo could find themselves under the baleful gaze of COINTELPRO.

The Black Panther Party, for example, was especially singled out. Their breakfast program, which served free breakfast to children in poor neighborhoods, was depicted as a sinister plot. FBI agents infiltrated the party, creating distrust and chaos from within. They sowed seeds of discord, leading to deadly shootouts between different Panther groups. And ordinary citizens who simply protested the Vietnam War were also targeted using a range of tactics, from sending fake letters to creating paranoia about communist infiltrators, to disrupting and discrediting these movements.

COINTELPRO was not some low-level operation either. It was spearheaded by the director of the FBI himself, J. Edgar Hoover, and had the blessing of top-tier government officials. In fact, it was so secretive that even high-ranking FBI officials were unaware of the extent of its operations.

It was Hoover who singled out King as a major target for COINTELPRO operations, which led the program's director to write in a report: "In the light of King's powerful demagogic speech ... We must mark him now if we have not done so before, as the most dangerous Negro of the future in this nation from the standpoint of communism, the Negro, and national security."

A Senate committee that later investigated COINTELPRO concluded that the program "began in 1956, in part because of frustration with Supreme Court rulings limiting the government's power to proceed overtly against dissident groups." In other words, since government officials were restrained in overt (direct and transparent) efforts, they resorted to covert (conspiratorial) efforts instead. When told that they couldn't violate people's rights, they decided to do it anyway, but secretly.

Cui Bono?

Obviously, the FBI and the broader US government profited immensely from COINTELPRO by maintaining their preferred societal structure and narrative. This was the era of the Cold War. Fear of communism was rampant, and anyone proposing changes to the status quo was seen as a potential Communist, a threat to the "American way of life." Under Hoover's leadership, the FBI took the reins in guarding this American narrative by discrediting and disrupting the groups they targeted, effectively neutralizing many individuals and organizations that they saw as a challenge to established order.

Consider the case of the Black Panther Party. The FBI's covert tactics created mistrust within the party, leading to infighting and public shootings. The ensuing chaos not only discredited the party but also diverted their efforts from community programs and political action into dealing with internal disputes. The government thus succeeded in mitigating a group they perceived as a "radical threat" to societal norms. The same goes for the civil rights movement and the anti-Vietnam War activists. By secretly casting these groups as dangerous and un-American, the FBI aimed to isolate them from mainstream society, diluting their impact and ensuring that the status quo prevailed.

While the FBI played the role of the puppet master, the media often acted as the puppet. Unwittingly or not, the media played a key role in propagating the FBI's narrative. Stories of infighting, allegations of criminal activities, and sordid personal details—whether true or fabricated—were lapped up by the media and presented to the public. This media manipulation further served the government's agenda by turning public opinion against these groups. COINTELPRO also benefited certain political entities and figures who were directly opposed to the values and changes proposed by these targeted groups.

These individuals and parties could continue their political agendas unchallenged, riding on the wave of public opinion shaped by the FBI's manipulations. In the end, the ones who truly profited were those who wanted to suppress dissent, stifle change, and keep the status quo intact.

Why Does This Matter?

Think for a moment why the government did this with King—a government that in theory is supposed to protect its citizens, not coerce and conspire against them. What does this behavior tell us about the government officials making those decisions—their intentions, their goals, and their views?

Certainly, those involved in this plot did not believe that all men are created equal, as King advocated. They believed, rather, in a system of elitism where some people control others—and they liked being at the top of the pyramid. People like King were the enemy—a threat to their power.

The legacy of COINTELPRO still echoes in today's world as the FBI continues to employ tactics just like those used decades ago. The Bureau's past activities, while criticized and condemned, are not merely historical footnotes—they form a consistent pattern of behavior that sadly (and secretly) continues today.

Consider the shocking announcement in October 2020, less than one month before a presidential election, revealing to the American public that the FBI had arrested thirteen people on charges of terrorism and conspiracy, with six of them accused of being part of a plot to kidnap the Michigan governor, Gretchen Whitmer, because of her heavy-handed COVID-19 lockdown measures.

The media pounced quickly after the FBI announcement, painting Trump and his supporters as domestic terrorists who were now resorting to new lows to punish their political adversaries. ABC News told viewers, "Tonight, we take you into a hidden world, a place authorities say gave birth to a violent domestic terror plot in Michigan—foiled by the FBI." MSNBC said, "The FBI thwarted what they described as a plot to violently overthrow the government and kidnap Michigan Gov. Gretchen Whitmer." CNN declared it "deeply alarming."

As later became clear, undercover FBI agents and informants were deeply embedded in the plot. One investigative report found that these federal agents were not just passive observers in a group of domestic terrorists, but proactive drivers of what they did—shaping almost every aspect of the alleged conspiracy. These revelations raised the troubling question: would there even have been a plot without FBI involvement and coordination?

The Whitmer case echoes previous FBI activities during the so-called "war on terror." Over and over again, the FBI was found to have been creating, funding, and driving many "terror plots" that they later claimed to have disrupted. The targets might be different—young American Muslims during the war on terror and young right-wing

White men in the Whitmer case—but the tactics remain disconcertingly similar. COINTELPRO was shut down in 1971, but the FBI's conspiratorial tactics continued under other program names—and still continue to this day.

What We Learned

1. COINTELPRO was shut down in 1971 but remains relevant today. The methods and tactics employed during this era continue to be mirrored in the FBI's current operations.

2. The FBI is not a passive observer of domestic problems—they are active instigators in trying to influence people's actions. This especially applies to people they perceive to be political dissenters or threats.

3. The lessons from the COINTELPRO era underscore the significant power that the FBI holds in shaping public narratives and political outcomes. This insight is crucial for understanding current political dynamics and the role of intelligence agencies.

Congressional Report

Final Report of the Select Committee to Study Government Operations with Respect to Intelligence Activities

April 26, 1976

Too many people have been spied upon by too many Government agencies and to much information has beeen collected. The Government has often undertaken the secret surveillance of citizens on the basis of their political beliefs, even when those beliefs posed no threat of violence or illegal acts on behalf of a hostile foreign power. The Government, operating primarily through secret informants, but also using other intrusive techniques such as wiretaps, microphone "bugs", surreptitious mail opening, and break-ins, has swept in vast amounts of information about the personal lives, views, and associations of American citizens.

Investigations of groups deemed potentially dangerous—and even of groups suspected of associating with potentially dangerous organizations—have continued for decades, despite the fact that those groups did not engage in unlawful activity. Groups and individuals have been harassed and disrupted because of their political views and their lifestyles. Investigations have been based upon vague standards whose breadth made excessive collection inevitable.

Unsavory and vicious tactics have been employed—including anonymous attempts to break up marriages, disrupt meetings, ostracize persons from their professions, and provoke target groups into rivalries that might result in deaths. Intelligence agencies have served the political and personal objectives of presidents and other high officials. While the agencies often committed excesses in response to pressure from high officials in the Executive branch and Congress, they also occasionally initiated improper activities and then concealed them from officials whom they had a duty to inform.

Governmental officials—including those whose principal duty is to enforce the law—have violated or ignored the law over long periods of time and have advocated and defended their right to break the law.

The Constitutional system of checks and balances has not adequately controlled intelligence activities. Until recently the Executive branch has neither delineated the scope of permissible activities nor established procedures for supervising intelligence agencies. Congress has failed to exercise sufficient oversight, seldom questioning the use to which its apropriations were being put. Most domestic intelligence issues have not reached the courts, and in those cases when they have reached the courts, the judiciary has been reluctant to grapple with them....

The FBI's COINTELPRO—counterintelligence program—was designed to "disrupt" groups and "neutralize" individuals deemed to be threats to domestic security. The FBI resorted to counterintelligence tactics in part because its chief officials believed that the existing law could not control the activities of certain dissident groups, and that court decisions had tied the hands of the intelligence community. Whatever opinion one holds about the policies of the targeted groups, many of the tactics employed by the FBI were indisputably degrading to a free society....

There has been, in short, a clear and sustained failure by those responsible to control the intelligence community and to ensure its accountability.

Russian Disinformation
FBI
CIA
BIDEN CAMPAIGN
No one may speak of this!
YOUR POST IS TAGGED FALSE.
YOUR VIDEO HAS BEEN TAKEN DOWN.
YOUR ACCOUNT IS PERMANENTLY SUSPENDED.

Hunter Biden's
LAPTOP

High-ranking government officials within the "intelligence" community used their influence to push a political agenda, manipulating narratives and controlling the flow of information.

As the 2020 presidential election campaign was reaching its climax, a controversial story broke that seemed to come straight out of a political thriller. At the center of the storm was a laptop, allegedly belonging to Hunter Biden, son of then-candidate Joe Biden. In October, just weeks before the election, the *New York Post* published a bombshell report claiming that a laptop, supposedly left by Hunter Biden at a repair shop, contained a trove of controversial emails and compromising personal content. These documents, the *Post* suggested, implicated both Hunter and his father in questionable overseas business dealings. The content of the laptop was portrayed as a potential game changer for the impending election.

It was a shocking revelation, but one that was immediately cast with doubt. Detractors pointed to the convoluted journey of the laptop—from a repair shop in Delaware to the *New York Post*'s news desk—as reason enough to question the legitimacy of the claims. The store owner's account of how the laptop landed in his shop, his inability to definitively identify Hunter Biden as the person who dropped it off, and his decision to make a copy of the hard drive and give it to Rudy Giuliani, President Trump's personal lawyer, only fueled the skepticism.

The types of content that the laptop was alleged to have contained—from compromising photos of Hunter Biden to supposedly incriminating emails linking Joe Biden to his son's business activities in Ukraine—were also considered by many as too sensational to be true. It was almost as if the laptop had been produced intentionally by someone as a political weapon, filled with exactly the type of damaging information that could hinder Joe Biden's presidential campaign.

Amidst the chaos and controversy, a consensus seemed to emerge among most of the media and many in the public: the laptop was a hoax, a political dirty trick, and perhaps even a piece of disinformation in a wider campaign to discredit Joe Biden and influence the election outcome. The narrative was set and widely reported: the laptop was nothing but a fake, a non-story that should not distract the public from the real issues at hand.

To that end, social media companies quickly censored the *Post*'s story. Twitter blocked users from sharing the link to the report. The platform even locked the *New York Post*'s official Twitter account, an unprecedented move against a major news publication. Facebook limited the distribution of the story on its platform, stating that the move was part of its standard process to reduce the spread of misinformation, pending fact-checking review. The story was viral on its own, and now the sudden efforts of social media companies to censor it raised further questions about what was really going on.

Things Aren't Always What They Seem

So why were media companies so quick to conclusively disagree with and suppress the *Post*'s story? Within a few days after the story was published, one of Biden's senior campaign officials reached out to former acting CIA Director Mike Morell to "help Biden." The idea was to create a letter saying that the damning emails on the laptop were Russian disinformation.

Over the next two days, Morell obtained signatures from

fifty-one former intelligence officials, including himself and four other former CIA directors. On October 19, five days after the story first broke, these officials published their letter, saying that their national security experience made them "deeply suspicious that the Russian government played a significant role" in producing the laptop for political purposes. They cited various examples from the news story that they said suggested Russia was to blame. "If we are right," they added, "this is Russia trying to influence how Americans vote in this election, and we believe strongly that Americans need to be aware of this."

Taking this to be true, media entities went into overdrive to suppress the story to contain the spread of Russian propaganda so as to protect the integrity of the election that was only days away. But the letter was a lie, and these officials did not believe that Russia was actually to blame.

Morell later revealed that he coordinated the letter to "help Vice President Biden… because I wanted him to win the election." An email he sent to one of his colleagues when asking for their signature showed that he said he was drafting the letter as a "talking point" for Joe Biden to use in his debate against President Trump—so that Biden could use the credibility of the intelligence community to discredit the laptop and its contents.

Cui Bono?

The media companies' haste to suppress the story raises questions about the true motivations behind their actions. Was this really an effort to combat disinformation, or was it more about shielding a political campaign from potential damage? The swift alignment of the media and the intelligence community served to quash the laptop story, depriving the public of a more swift search for the truth amid controversial allegations about corruption in the Biden family.

It's also worth noting that the intelligence community's decision to label the laptop as Russian disinformation was based on zero evidence. The eagerness to blame Russia and the quick agreement to sign the letter shortly after the news broke suggest that these officials were willing to dismiss unflattering revelations about their preferred presidential candidate without actually obtaining intelligence on the matter. It's clear that these officials, who wrap themselves in the cloak of caring about national security, were simply leveraging their professional credibility to advance a political agenda. It's likely that these individuals felt that Biden would not disrupt what they were trying to do, and therefore preferred him over President Trump.

It's also obvious that the Biden campaign was a primary beneficiary of the suppression and discrediting of the *New York Post*'s story. The emergence of potentially damaging information about Hunter Biden, just weeks before the election, posed a significant threat to Joe Biden's bid for presidency. The swift and sweeping discrediting of the story, supported by the intelligence community's letter, neutralized this threat, thereby benefiting the campaign.

It is also noteworthy to consider who didn't benefit from the suppression of the laptop story. The general public, who was shielded from supposed "disinformation," was instead kept in the dark about significant revelations about a presidential candidate's family. They were manipulated and lied to by officials with a political agenda, and the truth took much longer to emerge after being suppressed so strenuously.

Why Does This Matter?

The suppression and labeling of the laptop story as "disinformation," without evidence, is a reminder of the influence and power of so-called "intelligence" agencies, who shape public opinion and control narratives, effectively turning the wheels of politics in their favor.

This power of shaping public opinion isn't simply about controlling the flow of information. It's about influencing the very foundation upon which society is built—truth. In this light, the Hunter Biden laptop story isn't just about a political scandal. It's about the mechanisms through which power is consolidated and exercised, and the immense sway that intelligence agencies hold over our collective understanding of reality. When these officials speak, the media parrot their proclamations as unquestioning truth, even though in this case (and many others), it's false.

Consider this: Operation CHAOS saw the CIA covertly surveil anti-war activists in order to hopefully discredit them. The Iran-Contra Affair had intelligence agencies secretly selling arms to Iran to fund rebels in Nicaragua—altering the narrative of US involvement abroad. In the lead up to the Iraq War, officials falsely claimed that Saddam Hussein possessed Weapons of Mass Destruction to anger Americans and justify invasion of that country. The Pentagon Papers, revealed in 1971, exposed systematic government deception about the progress and objectives of the Vietnam

War to maintain public support. And in Operation Northwoods, mentioned previously, the Joint Chiefs of Staff of the US military proposed killing American citizens and falsely blaming it on Cuba in order to incite anger amongst the public to support intervening militarily. These and many more examples underscore just how intrusive intelligence agencies have been in shaping political narratives and public opinion.

The idea behind intelligence agencies is that they can gather information through various means and then inform government officials, and even the public, about the reality of a particular situation. In theory, they should be observational only, but in practice they have far exceeded what they were tasked to do, whether it be the FBI, CIA, NSA, or other government agencies. Ultimately, the Hunter Biden laptop story is an example of the famous quote from Lord Acton, "Power tends to corrupt and absolute power corrupts absolutely."

What We Learned

1. The Hunter Biden laptop controversy highlights how information can be manipulated for political gain. This was evident by how many media outlets, with the backing of intelligence community officials, dismissed the story as Russian disinformation without evidence to back up their claim.

2. Intelligence agencies, like the CIA, have been historically involved in swaying public opinion or influencing politics, sometimes by spreading disinformation themselves.

3. We need to verify information before accepting it as fact—especially when the information comes from government officials, who often lie. The letter from the former intelligence officials was initially accepted by many as truth, but the motives behind it were later revealed to be politically driven.

Request to Sign On to Statement

An email from former CIA Acting Director Mike Morell and a longtime CIA colleague, Marc Polymeropoulos, to fellow intelligence community officials

October 18, 2020

To all (everyone is on the bcc line to protect folks privacy):

Marc and I drafted the attached [coalition letter] because we believe the Russians were involved in some way in the Hunter Biden email issue and because we think Trump will attack Biden on the issue at this week's debate and we want to give the VP a talking point to use in response.

We would be honored if each of you would be willing to join us in signing the letter.

If you do agree to sign, please let me know how you would like your affiliation to read. For those CIA officers on the bcc line, I would like to find a way to highlight your Russia work, if appropriate....

If you want to agree to sign but make that **conditional** on seeing who else is willing to sign, I'm happy to send you the final list, probably tomorrow, before obtaining your final approval.

I will clear the statement with the Publication Review Board at CIA tomorrow.

Let us know. Thanks.

Michael and Marc

Peace is bad for business... I mean, American interests.
Yeah, maawrr warrr!

A New PEARL HARBOR

Most Americans were stunned as the horrific events of September 11, 2001, unfolded. Many theories emerged about what happened, so the government put out an official report to settle the debate. But the very people in charge of the report believe it isn't true...

REBUILDING AMERICA'S DEFENSES

Strategy, Forces and Resources For a New Century

A Report of
The Project for the New American Century
September 2000

Marcy Borders rode the elevator up to the 81st floor of the North Tower in the World Trade Center, heading to her office where she had recently started working as a clerical assistant. Just a few minutes later, an airplane crashed into the building just a few stories above her office. "My supervisor thought a small jet plane might have nipped us," she later said. "We had no idea what was going on."

"You felt the building shaking, you heard the explosion, you saw chairs coming out the windows, office supplies, [and] what I know now were people," Borders said. She joined countless others rushing for the exit staircase, cramming past tired firefighters working their way to the upper floors in search of anyone who might be trapped. Borders finally reached the bottom of the stairs, and at that moment, the South Tower collapsed, hitting her with a massive cloud of dust and debris.

"Once it caught me it threw me on my hands and knees. Every time I inhaled my mouth filled up with it," she explained. "I was saying to myself out loud, I didn't want to die, I didn't want to die." Borders didn't die—at least not right away. She died fourteen years later, at age forty-two, from stomach cancer that she believed was linked to the debris she breathed in on 9/11.

Nearly 3,000 people died in the attacks on that fateful day. There were 2,753 deaths at the World Trade Center site—and 343 of these were firefighters trying to rescue others. At the Pentagon, which had been struck by another plane, 184 people died. And 40 people died in Pennsylvania, where airplane passengers fought back against their hijackers, ultimately crashing the plane and killing everyone on board.

Americans and people all over the world were glued to their TVs, watching horrifying images of the plane attacks and the aftermath. Understandably, the key question lingering in the air was, "Why?" Why did these people attack us? It was clear that it was a coordinated effort, with multiple planes. But it was unclear why anyone would want to hurt us.

An answer was soon provided. President George W. Bush told the public that these terrorists and their supporters despise "individual choice—and thus they bear a special hatred for America." They "hate all civilization and culture and progress," he later said, and they are "devious and ruthless." Or, more simply, Bush separately said that the terrorists "hate us, because we're free." The 9/11 attack was repeatedly framed by the government as an unprovoked act of aggression from truly evil people who needed to be eradicated from whatever caves and holes they dwelled in.

And that was precisely what was soon proposed. Just three days after the attack, President Bush said that "Our responsibility to history is clear: to answer these attacks and rid the world of evil." He said that, "History has called America and our allies to action, and it is both our responsibility and our privilege to fight freedom's fight." War was the plan—not an attack on a country, but a fight against the very idea of "terror" and anyone who tried to inflict it on others.

To convince Americans to go along with war, Bush and his allies called to mind another time when America was suddenly attacked. "The events of September the 11th were as decisive as the attack on Pearl Harbor," he said. Just a few weeks after the attacks, the Deputy Secretary of Defense said:

> Until two months ago, the date most synonymous with surprise was December 7th. But as we mark the sixtieth anniversary of Pearl Harbor next month, we may also recall that Japan's attack drove us not to fear, but to action; not into isolation, but to accept a greater role in the world; not to forsake our friends, but to form with them the most powerful alliance against evil in history. December 7th was a turning point for the world, and September 11th should be no less a turning point. On 9/11, our generation received one of history's great wakeup calls. Like the Greatest Generation, we must answer that call.

And so, recalling the attack on Pearl Harbor decades prior, America went to war against "terror" throughout the Middle East, in direct response to the apparently unprovoked attack on American soil on September 11, 2001.

Things Aren't Always What They Seem

As it turns out, the 9/11 attacks did not occur because cave-dwelling terrorists half a world away "hate us because we're free." The coordinated attack was a response in retaliation to perceived injustices. Osama bin Laden, the founder of al-Qaeda which was responsible for the attacks, published a letter a year later where he explained in detail what motivated him and his associates.

"Why are we fighting and opposing you?" he wrote. "The

answer is very simple: Because you attacked us and continue to attack us." He then outlined several examples to justify his position:

> You attacked us in Palestine… which has sunk under military occupation for more than 80 years…
>
> You attacked us in Somalia; you supported the Russian atrocities against us in Chechnya, the Indian oppression against us in Kashmir, and the Jewish aggression against us in Lebanon.
>
> Under your supervision, consent and orders, the governments of our countries which act as your agents, attack us on a daily basis;
>
> You steal our wealth and oil at paltry prices because of you[r] international influence and military threats. This theft is indeed the biggest theft ever witnessed by mankind in the history of the world.
>
> Your forces occupy our countries; you spread your military bases throughout them; you corrupt our lands, and you besiege our sanctities, to protect the security of the Jews and to ensure the continuity of your pillage of our treasures.
>
> You have starved the Muslims of Iraq, where children die every day. It is a wonder that more than 1.5 million Iraqi children have died as a result of your sanctions, and you did not show concern. Yet when 3000 of your people died, the entire world rises and has not yet sat down.

"Is it in any way rational to expect that after America has attacked us for more than half a century," bin Laden wrote, "that we will then leave her to live in security and peace?!!" Of course, these ideas may be off base, exaggerated, or totally incorrect—and regardless, these views don't justify killing innocent people as bin Laden's allies in al-Qaeda did. But these arguments show he and his associates had specific objections that served as the basis for their anger. And the government knew of the likelihood of such an attack happening. The CIA had developed a term for it after they secretly overthrew the Iranian government in 1953: blowback. It was the recognition that meddling in other people's business would create negative consequences down the road. Chalmers Johnson, author of the book *Blowback*, observed how government officials made sure the public didn't understand what was happening, so that they could continue their foreign meddling:

> Actions that generate blowback are normally kept totally secret from the American public and from most of their representatives in Congress. This means that when innocent civilians become victims of a retaliatory strike, they are at first unable to put it in context or to understand the sequence of events that led up to it. In its most rigorous definition, blowback does not mean mere reactions to historical events but rather to clandestine operations carried out by the US government that are aimed at overthrowing foreign regimes, or seeking the execution of people the United States wants eliminated by "friendly" foreign armies, or helping launch state terrorist operations against overseas target populations. The American people may not know what is done in their name, but those on the receiving end surely do—including the people of Iran

(1953), Guatemala (1954), Cuba (1959 to the present), Congo (1960), Brazil (1964), Indonesia (1965), Vietnam (1961-73), Laos (1961-73), Cambodia (1961-73), Greece (1967-74), Chile (1973), Afghanistan (1979 to the present), El Salvador, Guatemala, and Nicaragua (1980s), and Iraq (1991 to the present), to name only the most obvious cases.

While most Americans were shocked by the 9/11 attacks, there were some who saw them as an opportunity they had been waiting for. Strangely, just a year prior to the 9/11 attacks, a group called the Project for a New American Century advocated for more military intervention abroad and the forcible removal of Saddam Hussein from power in Iraq—a "regime change." They published a lengthy paper in which they lamented that America's overseas interventions and military buildup would be too slow to respond strongly enough and assert continued American dominance across the globe. Reaching their goal of American imperialism "is likely to be a long one," they wrote, "absent some catastrophic and catalyzing event–like *a new Pearl Harbor.*"

One year later, this group had their opportunity—a "new Pearl Harbor." That Deputy Secretary of Defense quoted earlier, who compared 9/11 to Pearl Harbor? His name is Paul Wolfowitz, and he was a member of this group. So were Dick Cheney, Donald Rumsfeld, and others who became part of President Bush's administration to carry out the very warfare and military involvement that they had long desired and feared would otherwise be too slow in coming.

Odd, right? Because of circumstances such as this, some believe that the attacks on 9/11 were conducted with direct involvement of government officials. Others believe that the attacks were independently planned and coordinated, but that some government officials knew ahead of time what was going to happen and chose not to stop them. Many others still believe that the attacks were totally unprovoked, caught everyone off guard, and that we were simply attacked because Islamic terrorists hate American freedoms.

So what's the truth? These insiders certainly took advantage of an attack to further their political goals of military domination. But there are other odd things that happened involving 9/11 which have led many people to suspect that what they've been told isn't the full picture. Consider a few examples:

- **Stock Market Trades.** Just days prior to 9/11, someone placed a huge bet in the stock market against American Airlines and United Airlines, so that they would make money if the stock price went down. After the attack, the stock prices for these two companies plummeted, making millions of dollars for whoever was doing the unusual trades. A government investigation into this "insider trading" yielded no results and no arrests.

- **Multiple Warnings.** Numerous intelligence reports warned government officials of what was about to happen, but those reports were apparently ignored. Italian intelligence warned that al-Qaeda was going to use aircraft to launch an attack. The Egyptians warned the

CIA that al-Qaeda members were in the United States being trained on how to fly planes. Israel's intelligence agency warned of nineteen terrorists in the United States who were planning to carry out an attack soon. Just weeks prior to the attack, the United Kingdom warned the United States three times of an imminent attack involving airplane hijackings.

- **Able Danger.** In 1999, the US government launched a classified military intelligence program known as "Able Danger" to target al-Qaeda and gather information on the activities of its members. This team apparently identified two of the three terrorist cells that later participated in the 9/11 attacks. That knowledge was mysteriously not acted upon, and when it was later investigated, officials at the Defense Intelligence Agency destroyed their data and documents to hide what they were up to. They also prohibited some of their key personnel from testifying to Congress, after initially denying that the program even existed.

- **Standing Orders.** As the third hijacked plane approached the Pentagon, President Bush was airborne in Air Force One. Vice President Dick Cheney (a founding member of the Project for a New American Century mentioned earlier) was in a command bunker. As the Pentagon-bound plane was still approaching, Cheney was warned of its close proximity. "The plane is 50 miles out. The plane is 30 miles out," a junior officer repeatedly reported. When he said, "The plane is 10 miles out," the young man asked the vice president, "Do the orders still stand?" Cheney replied, "Of course the orders still stand. Have you heard anything to the contrary?" Since Bush later issued an order to shoot down problematic planes, it seems that this order was to not shoot these planes down. Though they had clear warnings, Cheney and the command center evidently chose not to respond as the Pentagon was struck.

- **Pentagon Corruption.** One day before the 9/11 attacks, the Secretary of Defense, Donald Rumsfeld (also a founding member of the Project for a New American Century), held a press conference over "a matter of life and death," as he called it. He revealed that $2.3 trillion (that's trillion with a 'T') had gone missing. And just hours later, the Pentagon was struck on the section of the building that contained the accounting offices, destroying all the documents needed to trace the missing money.

- **WTC7.** Few people are aware that a third tower fell at the World Trade Center on 9/11. Tower 7, which was not hit by a plane, and which was a full city block away from the twin towers, collapsed that afternoon. A government report claimed that "WTC 7 collapsed because of fires fueled by office furnishings" as a result of debris from one of the twin towers. Tower 7 fell into its own footprint at near-free-fall speed—a remarkable feat for a steel structure. After the fires had raged for hours, the owner of the building, Larry Silverstein, said, "The smartest thing to do is pull it"—an apparent reference to controlled demolition. "And they made that decision to pull and we watched the building collapse," he said. This contradicts the official narrative and suggests a possible ulterior motive in the destruction of the tower or the documents and evidence contained in its offices.

There are certainly more unusual circumstances and unanswered questions. To address the public's concerns, the government created the National Commission on Terrorist Attacks Upon the United States, also known as the 9/11 Commission. After hearing extensive testimony from key witnesses, the Commission produced a 585 page report—the official narrative on what happened that fateful day. Yet, the report didn't mention Tower 7 at all. Able Danger was missing from its pages as well. The testimony about Dick Cheney's actions in the command center as the plane struck the Pentagon was ignored. And the Commission's own members don't even believe the report is accurate. The chair and vice chair argue that they were "set up to fail," denied the funding they needed to perform a thorough investigation, and given an unreasonably limited timeline to sift through millions of documents and interview hundreds of key witnesses. They admit they were denied access to the truth and lied to by high-ranking officials. "The chief obstacle," the chair and vice chair later argued, "was the White House."

After initially resisting testifying before the Commission, President Bush and Vice President Cheney agreed to be interviewed—but only if they were together. This, of course, is a highly unusual way of questioning a key witness during an investigation and was likely done so that the two of them could stay on the same page and not say anything contradictory.

And the CIA director refused to allow the Commission to interview terrorist detainees. The Commission's chair was shocked a few years later when learning that the CIA had actually destroyed the video recordings of their interrogations of these detainees—shocked not merely by their destruction of this evidence, but more shocked to even learn that these video recordings existed. The Commission was never given the evidence during their investigations.

Many questions remain unanswered because of the cover-up by government officials, the destruction of evidence, and the refusal to testify and thoroughly investigate. What *is* a clear conspiracy is the coordinated effort to keep the public from understanding why the attack really happened. The militaristic desires of the Bush administration—heavily staffed with people who had previously advocated for increasing intervention into Iraq and the Middle East—required painting America as a hapless victim of "terror" without giving the public any context that might show that this attack was an intentional retaliation for the US military's past meddling abroad. It was a conspiracy, then, to take advantage of the fear Americans felt and the revenge they desired in order to kickstart years of warfare to reshape the geopolitical landscape.

Cui Bono?

President Bush's administration was heavily composed of neoconservatives—people who favor heavy military intervention abroad. These individuals wanted to continue dictating what would happen in other countries in order to control their resources and governments. Many of these individuals were open about their desires, such as the members of the Project for a New American Century. They clearly benefited from the attacks on 9/11 since Americans began demanding the very thing they wanted—a military escalation in response. They now had positions of political influence in the Bush administration to carry out the very policies for which they had been advocating.

Another beneficiary of the 9/11 attacks was the Military-Industrial Complex—a term used to describe the tight-knit relationship between a nation's military leadership and the industries that support them. In the United States, this refers to the Department of Defense, the armed forces (the Army, Navy, Air Force, Marines, and Coast Guard), and the industries that make all the stuff they use—think tanks, battleships, jets, missiles, and more. These companies literally profit off of war and, therefore, desire more of it; battles are good for business. Since 9/11, these private companies have received trillions of dollars from the Pentagon. And they spend tens of millions of dollars each year lobbying elected officials and contributing to their campaigns, hoping to curry favor with politicians who will keep the war machine alive to boost their profits.

In his farewell address as he left office, President Dwight D. Eisenhower—who previously served as the Supreme Commander of the Allied Expeditionary Forces in Europe during World War II—warned Americans about the Military-Industrial Complex. "Only an alert and knowledgeable citizenry," he said, "can compel the proper meshing of the huge industrial and military machinery of defense with our peaceful methods and goals, so that security and liberty may prosper together." But consider Donald Rumsfeld's admission about $2.3 trillion missing at the Pentagon and the highly convenient attack the following day that destroyed the very records that might reveal the source of the corruption. There can't be an alert and knowledgeable citizenry if they are deprived of information and truth—just as the 9/11 Commission, tasked with reporting the truth, was repeatedly deprived of the information necessary to understand what actually happened. Certainly, the government officials involved in using all this taxpayer money—likely for "black ops" that they didn't want Congress and the public to know about—benefited from the Pentagon attack that destroyed the evidence and distracted the public from Rumsfeld's press conference.

The 9/11 attacks benefited al-Qaeda as well. Certainly the incident aligned with their objectives to punish the United States, but the US response to the attacks—launching the war on terror and bombing cities in Afghanistan, Iraq, and elsewhere in the Middle East—also helped them grow stronger. As thet war created carnage and killed or displaced countless innocent bystanders, many angry men seeking revenge joined al-Qaeda's ranks to fight the enemy. This is the "blowback" concept the CIA identified after their foreign meddling half a century prior.

Why Does This Matter?

After two decades of waging a "war on terror," the military's actions siphoned $8 trillion in taxpayer dollars and caused 900,000 deaths. That figure does not include all the many deaths caused indirectly by way of disease, displacement, or deprivation of food and clean water. Over 37 million people fled their homes as a result of the warfare. This massive disruption and destruction is the consequence of what many in the Bush administration—particularly the members of the Project for a New American Century—had wanted; it's one thing to express a desire for regime change in another country, and another thing to actually make it happen and harm and kill many innocent people along the way.

What happened on 9/11 also matters because it was a huge inflection point in our society. Americans were terrified by terrorists, and in their fear, they surrendered their freedoms to a government that began growing in size and power. Instead of passing a declaration of war as required by the Constitution, Congress simply authorized the president to wage the war he thought necessary to "fight terror." This set a dangerous precedent for expansion of power in the executive branch and the abandonment of Congress's oversight duty.

In response to 9/11, the government also enacted the deceptively-titled USA PATRIOT Act (the Uniting and Strengthening America by Providing Appropriate Tools Required to Intercept and Obstruct Terrorism Act). This sweeping legislation radically expanded the government's ability to conduct surveillance on individuals without judicial oversight, including Americans not suspected of committing a crime. The government also created the Department of Homeland Security, including the Transportation Security Administration, to invasively screen airplane passengers in the name of safety. These actions have normalized the invasion of our privacy, making Americans accustomed to surrendering their freedom in exchange for a feeling of security.

Ignoring President Eisenhower's warning, Americans have been unwilling or unable to restrain the growth of the Military-Industrial Complex. In a post-9/11 world, the US military budget is bigger than the military budgets of the next largest eleven countries combined. Trillions of dollars have been siphoned away to for-profit defense contractors who are incentivized to continue to increase their production of equipment and weapons. And as the military's foreign footprint grew, the escalation of war trickled down to thousands of local law enforcement agencies who became militarized after being given extra or used military equipment—armored vehicles, grenade launchers, machine guns, helicopters, and more. This transformed the relationship between the citizenry and those hired to protect them, leading to more people being hurt and killed because of excessive force being utilized by the militarized police.

Eisenhower warned of "the potential for the disastrous rise of misplaced power" if the Military-Industrial Complex were to grow. And 9/11 was a spark that lit a fire—one whose flames were fanned by neoconservatives to push for war and greater American authority across the globe. For example, one military general, Wesley Clark, learned of a memo just days after the 9/11 attacks that outlined a strategy to invade seven countries in five years!

It's possible that some government officials had advance knowledge of the impending plane hijackings. It's also possible that al-Qaeda legitimately caught everyone in the US government off guard. But what's clear is that the 9/11 attacks are still shrouded in mystery as a result of destroyed records, lying government officials, political cover-ups, and an official report that has been rejected by the very people who helped create it.

What We Learned

1. It's difficult to put theories to rest and conclusively state what happened when the public has been deprived of access to critical evidence and information. Even the Commission members tasked with finding out the truth of what all happened on 9/11 were lied to, denied access, and ultimately concluded that their official report was not accurate.

2. The way an event is framed by those in power can greatly impact its interpretation. Removing context from the 9/11 attack—making sure Americans didn't know that it was a response to their government's foreign meddling abroad—makes it easier to persuade people that they were attacked because of their core freedoms and national identity. This then makes it easier to manipulate them, such as convincing them of the need for a full-blown "war on terror" to respond to the atrocity.

3. When a crisis happens, those in power are quick to respond with proposals that expand their power further. And while these new programs and laws are initially aimed at the original problem (in this case combating terrorism), they are often later turned inward on the American people.

4. The Military-Industrial Complex has become stronger than ever in a post-9/11 world, suggesting that Eisenhower's warning fell on deaf ears.

Rebuilding America's Defenses

Excerpt of a Report of the
Project for a New American Century

September 2000

To preserve American military preeminence in the coming decades, the Department of Defense must move more aggressively to experiment with new technologies and operational concepts, and seek to exploit the emerging revolution in military affairs. Information technologies, in particular, are becoming more prevalent and significant components of modern military systems. These information technologies are having the same kind of transforming effects on military affairs as they are having in the larger world. The effects of this military transformation will have profound implications for how wars are fought, what kinds of weapons will dominate the battlefield and, inevitably, which nations enjoy military preeminence.

The United States enjoys every prospect of leading this transformation. Indeed, it was the improvements in capabilities acquired during the American defense buildup of the 1980s that hinted at and then confirmed, during Operation Desert Storm, that a revolution in military affairs was at hand. At the same time, the process of military transformation will present opportunities for America's adversaries to develop new capabilities that in turn will create new challenges for U.S. military preeminence....

Any serious effort at transformation must occur within the larger framework of U.S. national security strategy, military missions and defense budgets. The United States cannot simply declare a "strategic pause" while experimenting with new technologies and operational concepts. Nor can it choose to pursue a transformation strategy that would decouple American and allied interests. A transformation strategy that solely pursued capabilities for projecting force from the United States, for example, and sacrificed forward basing and presence, would be at odds with larger American policy goals and would trouble American allies.

Further, the process of transformation, even if it brings revolutionary change, is likely to be a long one, absent some catastrophic and catalyzing event — **like a new Pearl Harbor**. Domestic politics and industrial policy will shape the pace and content of transformation as much as the requirements of current missions. A decision to suspend or terminate aircraft carrier production, as recommended by this report and as justified by the clear direction of military technology, will cause great upheaval....

Only such a force posture, service structure and level of defense spending will provide America and its leaders with a variety of forces to meet the strategic demands of the world's sole superpower. Keeping the American peace requires the U.S. military to undertake a broad array of missions today and rise to very different challenges tomorrow, but there can be no retreat from these missions without compromising American leadership and the benevolent order it secures. This is the choice we face. It is not a choice between preeminence today and preeminence tomorrow. Global leadership is not something exercised at our leisure, when the mood strikes us or when our core national security interests are directly threatened; then it is already too late. Rather, it is a choice whether or not to maintain American military preeminence, to secure American geopolitical leadership, and to preserve the American peace.

Look, Reginald. It appears the banking interests have agreed upon a scheme for world domination...
Welcome to the Jekyll Island Club

The Creature from
JEKYLL ISLAND

Presented as a way to make the economy less turbulent, a secret group's proposal to create a central bank in the US ended up making more economic problems while enriching the bankers and politicians who had access to its money machine.

In the early 1900s, the US economy was kind of like a roller coaster ride—thrilling at times, but also packed with perilous ups and downs. You never knew when the next drop was coming, and when it hit, it hit hard. One such downturn was the Panic of 1907, a financial crisis that saw stock prices plummet and banks crumble. It was like an economic earthquake that sent shockwaves across the country. People were withdrawing their money from the banks, causing them to go out of business—and the panic only ended when J.P. Morgan, an extremely wealthy banker, gathered some fellow banking magnates to pool their resources, take over some failing banks, and calm the nerves of the public.

Many people who fell victim to this economic turbulence began to question whether a free-market economy, left to its own devices, was really the best way to go. Sure, it had its benefits, like promoting competition and innovation, but it also had a knack for creating financial instability. People's livelihoods were at stake! They didn't want to keep living in fear of the next financial disaster. These concerned citizens felt that something had to be done to stabilize the economic seesaw.

And so, a group of well-intentioned leaders decided to craft a proposal that would restructure America's economy to give it a firmer footing that would minimize or eliminate the huge up-and-down swings. They believed they had the perfect plan to put the brakes on this financial roller coaster and solicited public input throughout the process to refine their thoughts and get buy-in from others. Their idea? To create a central banking system—a sort of financial referee—to keep things in check. This new system would help manage the country's money supply, stabilize prices, and stop bank failures. It would be like a protective shield, guarding the economy against future crises. They called it the Federal Reserve.

Things Aren't Always What They Seem

In reality, this group did not operate transparently or solicit public input. Their efforts were instead shrouded in secrecy. Senator Nelson Aldrich, chairman of the Senate finance committee, felt strongly that the United States needed a central bank in order to prevent future banking panics. So, he organized a trip disguised as a duck hunting expedition to Jekyll Island, an island off the coast of Georgia. This island had a fancy resort where J.P. Morgan, who was co-owner and a member, made sure no one else would be present.

Aldrich—one of the most powerful men in Washington, DC, and an investment associate of J.P. Morgan's—invited a few New York bankers and the assistant secretary of the treasury to this secret meeting and instructed them each to board a train, one by one, in New Jersey. Waiting for them there would be Aldrich's fancy private rail car, hitched to the end, ready to transport them on a thousand-mile journey to Georgia. Aldrich told each invitee to use only their first names and to dress up in hunting clothing to conceal their true identities and support the cover story pitched to the press—that Aldrich and some friends were going duck hunting. Some of the group chose new first names for their temporary identity instead of using their own.

While Aldrich was easily recognized by most of the gathered passengers waiting to board their train, his guests were not. By arriving separately, they would avoid attracting the attention of any reporters in the area; Aldrich had also said that if they encountered one another inside the train station, they should pretend they didn't know who the other person was. Not even the servants and service people on the train knew their identities. Their railroad car was kept dark and blocked off from other passengers, including reporters. The Georgia-bound group included:

1. Senator Nelson Aldrich: chairman of the Senate finance committee; chairman of the National Monetary Commission; investment associate of J.P. Morgan; father-in-law to business magnate John D. Rockefeller Jr.

2. Abraham Andrew: assistant secretary of the United States Treasury.

3. Frank Vanderlip: president of the National City Bank of New York, the most powerful bank; confidant of the Rockefellers.

4. Henry Davison: senior partner at the J.P. Morgan Company.

5. Charles Norton: president of J.P. Morgan's First National Bank of New York.

6. Benjamin Strong: head of J.P. Morgan's Bankers Trust Company.

7. Paul Warburg: partner in Kuhn, Loeb & Company, a large investment bank; representative of the Rothschild banking dynasty; brother to Max Warburg, head of the Warburg banking consortium in Europe.

These men, who together represented an estimated one-fourth of the world's wealth, spent the next week isolated in the Jekyll Island Club, working together to outline a central bank system that they could then get passed through Congress, using Aldrich's influence. Their efforts were secretive in part because Americans were deeply skeptical of both powerful banks and centralization of authority—so a "central bank" was hardly music to their ears. And their skepticism wasn't new; Alexander Hamilton's proposed Bank of the United States, modeled after the Bank of England, started operating in 1791 with a twenty-year charter. When its charter came up for renewal, Congress barely shot it down by one vote in each chamber; Thomas Jefferson and his political allies argued that the Constitution didn't grant Congress the authority to charter a national bank, and that only the states could do so.

A few years later, after the War of 1812, Congress decided to try again and chartered the Second Bank of the United States. When its twenty-year charter came up for renewal, Congress gave it their approval, but President Andrew Jackson vetoed it. And then a few years later, Congress tried once more with a third bank, but President John Tyler also vetoed it. The deep suspicion many felt towards big banks was observed by Alexis de Tocqueville who wrote, "Americans are obviously preoccupied by one great fear"—when power "tends to become concentrated in a few hands," or what he called "centralization."

Thus, secrecy was necessary to hammer out something that ran afoul of American interests—the creation of a centralized banking cartel that would enrich the politically connected at the expense of everyone else. Warburg, one of the attendees, wrote nearly two decades later that, "The results of the conference were entirely confidential. Even the fact there had been a meeting was not permitted to become public." He added, "Though eighteen years have since gone by, I do not feel free to give a description of this most interesting conference concerning which Senator Aldrich pledged all participants to secrecy." Frank Vanderlip, another attendee, later admitted why the secrecy was so significant:

> Despite my views about the value to society of greater publicity for the affairs of corporations, there was an occasion, near the close of 1910, when I was as secretive—indeed, as furtive—as any conspirator... I do not feel it is any exaggeration to speak of our secret expedition to Jekyll Island as the occasion of the actual conception of what eventually became the Federal Reserve System...
>
> The servants and train crew may have known the identities of one or two of us, but they did not know all, and it was the names of all printed together that would have made our mysterious journey significant in Washington, in Wall Street, even in London. Discovery, we knew, simply must not happen, or else all our time and effort would be wasted. If it were to be exposed publicly that our particular group had got together and written a banking bill, that bill would have no chance whatever of passage by Congress.

Despite their conspiratorial efforts to increase their chances of success, the Aldrich plan failed in Congress. Changing political winds in the next election meant that Aldrich's association to the bill became a hindrance rather than a help; with the Democrats now in control of the federal government, these bankers made some tweaks and presented the proposal as a Democratic measure. As Vanderlip wrote, "Although the Aldrich Federal Reserve Plan was defeated when it bore the name Aldrich, nevertheless its essential points were all contained in the plan that was finally adopted." Once Congress finally passed the bill, with President Woodrow Wilson signing it into law, the banking elite were beside themselves. The President of Chase National Bank boastfully told his fellow bankers that the proposal would "make all incorporated banks together joint owners of a central dominating power."

Key to their strategy was appealing to the American desire for decentralization by portraying the Federal Reserve not as a single, monolithic bank, but as a network of central banks scattered across the country. There would be twelve of them, each privately owned by other banks and overseen by the Federal Reserve Board of Governors, who would be nominated by the President to serve a term of fourteen years upon being confirmed by the Senate. It would stabilize the economy and keep inflation at bay.

At least, that was the marketing message used to sell the public on the idea. In reality, the Federal Reserve made the economic roller coaster an even bumpier and more dangerous ride. It presided over a number of market crashes and recessions as well as the Great Depression in the 1930s. It has created so much new money out of thin air that it has destroyed well over 95 percent of the dollar's purchasing power. It was presented as a way to create market stability when in reality it has simply been a sneaky shell game to transfer wealth from Americans to the political elite by allowing them to access and spend newly created money before the effects of its inflation were felt by others, causing prices to rise.

Cui Bono?

After the banking panic of 1907, Vanderlip had complained to his fellow bankers that in times of economic struggle, "Each institution stands alone, concerned first with its own safety, and using every endeavor to pile up reserves without regard" to how their selfish actions were affecting other banks. He was complaining about competition—having some banks suffer while others succeeded. Each of America's nearly 15,000 banks were competing for control of cash, trying to win customers and provide services that would empower them to grow and succeed. But this was loathsome to folks like Vanderlip who seek to use the power of government to discourage competition. Thus, Vanderlip found himself at the Jekyll Island Club Resort with a few like-minded protectionists who together outlined the plan for a banking cartel in America.

There were (and are) three main groups who benefited from the creation of the Federal Reserve. The first is the large banks and financial institutions who are able to engage in risky investments and loans because of the Fed's role as the "lender of last resort," where it will loan banks money to bail them out of bad decisions if they are unable to obtain a loan anywhere else. This guarantee effectively shields banks from the consequences of their own actions, thus incentivizing them to make riskier decisions where they otherwise would show restraint.

The second group is the government. In order to fund its large projects and programs, the government sells bonds—an IOU where it promises to pay in the future for the money it receives today. The Fed buys this debt from the government, creating an eager customer who is willing to finance the government's largesse. This creates an incentive for politicians to spend money (to try and win votes) instead of having to worry about balancing the budget and only spending what the government collected in taxes. If the Fed has an unlimited checking account (because it can create new money out of thin air), then it can continue to buy all the debt the government wants to issue.

Another group that benefits is companies and consumers who desire cheap credit—low interest rates. In a free market, the interest rate moves up and down depending on a variety of factors. But the Federal Reserve arbitrarily controls the interest rate and dictates how much interest banks will be able to charge on loans like home mortgages. With higher rates, people are incentivized to save money and earn interest on their savings. But when interest rates are kept low artificially, this encourages companies and individuals to purchase new things using cheap credit, deferring the payments until a later date since the interest rates are so low. This creates malinvestment and risky behavior because cheap credit encourages people to go into debt. In turn, the banks love this because they're able to profit by issuing so many loans to people.

Why Does This Matter?

Do you have a job yet, or another way to earn income? Chances are that you are a very jealous guardian of your hard-earned money. You probably winced when you saw your first pay stub and how much was being taken out for taxes. You spend wisely what you've worked so hard to earn. But what if you knew that your money would be worthless next month? Would you save it for a future, large purchase? Probably not—you'd do the wise thing and spend it while it had some value.

This scenario has played out for hundreds of millions of people in recent decades. Because the Federal Reserve creates new money (not backed by gold or another asset), that means that all the existing dollars in circulation become worth less. And that's why, since the Federal Reserve was created, the dollar has lost a whopping 95 percent of its value!

Ask your grandparents what a candy bar cost when they were your age, and you'll immediately see what happens over time when a central bank controls currency like this. Basically, your money is being stolen—its value transferred to bankers and politicians who can use the newly printed money before inflation's effects are felt by rising prices.

Ultimately, the institutions that control money control people. That's because money just represents our time and energy. You go to work to earn money, and then you can store up that energy you spent working into the money you get. When you're ready, you can release some of your energy by spending some of the money. What's in your wallet, then, is part of you. And when that money is manipulated, *you're* being manipulated. If other people can cut the power of your money in half (by printing a lot more of it), then they're basically stealing half of your energy that you stored up.

We're told today, as we have been for decades, that the Federal Reserve is a critical institution to manage our economy—that it tries to keep inflation low and help banks in need. But the Federal Reserve hasn't kept inflation low at all—quite the opposite, in fact. It is responsible for creating untold economic carnage. Its board of bankers don't know how to control the economy—no one does! But they despise a free market of competition and thus want to keep the banking cartel tightly knit in order to preserve their economic and political power.

If you care about freedom, you have to care about the impact of the Federal Reserve. It is the chief reason why the government has grown so large, financed by all the debt sold to the central bank. Under a gold standard, or some other restrictive system, the government would have to directly tax people in order to raise revenue. But with the Federal Reserve printing up new money, the government can both tax people directly and also tax them indirectly by inflating the money supply and using newly created money to pay the bills.

What We Learned

1. When there are problems, conniving people will push their preferred solution as the "fix" to resolve the problem. That happened with the Panic of 1907 and the banking crisis, which led powerful people to conspire and create a central bank in the United States.

2. Those who want to achieve something that the public is largely against will often conspire in secret to design their plans and determine how they can manipulate

the public into supporting them. The secretive nature of the Jekyll Island trip is another example of this common trend.

3. The Federal Reserve's ability to create new money has led to the devaluation of the dollar, where it has lost over 95 percent of its value.

4. The government has grown as big as it has because it is able to incur debt that the Federal Reserve will buy, providing it an endless supply of dollars to finance programs that it doesn't have enough tax revenue to cover.

The First Public Report

Excerpts of a news report from Bertie Charles Forbes (who later founded *Forbes* magazine)

October 19, 1916

Picture a party of the nation's greatest bankers stealing out of New York on a private railroad car under cover of darkness, stealthily hieing hundreds of miles South, embarking on a mysterious launch, sneaking on to an island deserted by all but a few servants, living there a full week under such rigid secrecy that the name of not one of them was once mentioned lest the servitors learn their indentity and disclose to the world this strangest, most secret eposide in the history of American finance.

I am not romancing. I am giving to the world, for the first time, the real story of how the famous Aldrich currency report, the foundation of our new currency system, was written....

The utmost secrecy was enjoined upon all. The public must not glean a hint of what was to be done. Senator Aldrich notified each one to go quietly into a private car which the railroad had received orders to draw up at an unfrequented platform. Drawn blinds balked any peering eyes that might be around. Off the party set. New York's ubiquitous reporters had been foiled....

[Senator Aldrich] had meanwhile confided to Harry, Frank, Paul and Piatt that he was to keep them locked up on Jekyll Island, cut off from the rest of the world, until they had evolved and compiled a scientific currency system for the United States.

So what do you think? It's pretty crazy to learn about all the awful and manipulative things governments and powerful people do to advance their agendas, isn't it?

It's easy to get discouraged when you read stories like these. You might even wonder what the point of learning about all these true conspiracies is when there's often little that the average person could have done to stop them while they were happening, since they were kept secret by those in power. The thing about conspiracies like these is that most people who are hurt by them have no idea anything suspicious is even happening at the time. But something that most of these stories have in common is that one or two people start noticing that something just doesn't seem right—they start asking questions, speaking out, and digging around to get to the bottom of what's really going on. And that's a really important thing to learn.

We can't change the bad things that governments have done in the past, but we can sure start paying attention to the things that are happening now. Knowing all of these stories helps us to see the world just a little bit differently. We don't need to walk around afraid, but we can certainly start listening to the news with an ear searching for hints of manipulation; we can start paying attention when it seems like movies, music, and other media are all trying to get us to think the same way about something, and we can talk to our friends and family about why that might be happening. We can ask questions and be skeptical of the "news" to try and figure out what's actually true.

For a long time, politicians and the media have smeared people as "conspiracy theorists" for challenging the official narrative of a particular event. And, of course, not every theory is true—there are some wild (and untrue) theories out there! But when the government has proven so many times that they do shady and conspiratorial things, it's clear that many "conspiracy theorists" were actually correct. So keep questioning, keep digging for truth when things don't add up, and keep trusting your gut when something just doesn't feel right. Who knows, maybe you'll uncover the next big true conspiracy!

—The Tuttle Twins